CHURCH CULTURE

CHURCH CULTURE

How to Assess It,
Shift It, and
Shape It

Jim Ozier and Yvette Thibodeaux

Abingdon Press

Nashville

CHURCH CULTURE:
HOW TO ASSESS IT, SHIFT IT, AND SHAPE IT

Copyright © 2024 by Abingdon Press

ISBN: 9781791033842
Library of Congress Control Number: 2024942194

Scripture quotations unless noted otherwise are from the Common English Bible. Copyright © 2011 by the Common English Bible. All rights reserved. Used by permission. www.CommonEnglishBible.com.

Scripture quotations marked NRSVue are taken from the New Revised Standard Version Updated Edition. Copyright © 2021 National Council of Churches of Christ in the United States of America. Used by permission. All rights reserved worldwide.

All diagrams were created by Liliana Rangel, team member at Church Difference Makers.

MANUFACTURED IN THE UNITED STATES OF AMERICA

Contents

Contents

PART 3. Building Your Church Culture Team

Find additional resource tools, The Complete Culture
Audit and Eleven Laws of Church Culture, online at
www.abingdonpress.com/culture-extras.

Foreword

By Jim Chandler, Chief Strategist, Difference Makers Group

For fun, I ride a Harley-Davidson motorcycle. As my wife and I travel the beautiful roadways along the Blue Ridge Mountains near our home just outside Charlottesville, Virginia, we pass through areas rich in history related to the formation of our nation. Not far from where we live is a specific designated national heritage area that is 180 miles long and 75 miles wide that stretches from Gettysburg, Pennsylvania, to Thomas Jefferson's home in Charlottesville. Along the roadways in this area are signs that read, "Journey through Hallowed Grounds."

To our team at the Difference Makers Group, culture change is always a sacred journey.

Changing the culture is not a leisurely Sunday afternoon drive through pleasant scenery in the comfort of "we've always done it this way." Instead, it is often a wild and unpredictable trip into places unknown and yet to be explored. It can be full of exhilaration and risks, detours and setbacks, dangers and thrills. Hey, that sounds like some of our trips on the Harley!

Changing the culture can be hard, but it doesn't have to be brutal. Chances are, many people over multiple generations have built your church. The invitation to change your culture is not an invitation to trash what exists and what has been or to treat it dismissively. Travel the road on which you are about to embark with an inspiring vision for the future, yes, but also with reverence for what God and God's people have done in the past.

In the pages that follow, my friends and colleagues Jim Ozier and Yvette Thibodeaux will take you on a deep dive into this short course on church culture. You will learn why church culture is the key to growth, vitality, and health. You will learn how to assess your church's existing culture and how to create and sustain the kind of culture needed to increase your church's impact in a fast-moving, ever-changing, and sometimes scary world.

Before you get started, let me add one final important thing to note. I have learned from a lot of great instructors over the years as I have worked to become a better and safer motorcycle rider. All the great instructors emphasize the dangers of something called "target fixation." Here is how target fixation works: When there is an obstacle in a rider's path, their natural instinct is to focus on the obstacle so they will not hit it. Makes perfect sense, right? Well, not so fast. The reality is that when a rider locks their focus on the obstacle—when they fixate on the target—they will actually steer toward the obstacle instead of away from it, often resulting in what we riders call "a bad day."

This is a book about your organizational culture. But be cautious not to get target fixation and obsess only about your church's culture. Appropriate systems, infrastructure, and ministry practices are needed to bring your culture to life. Culture without systems leads only to spinning your wheels and heading for a crash.

We at the Difference Makers Group are culture geeks. We are quite convinced that culture is the primary thing in growing the health and influence of your church, but we know it is not the only thing. I hope you will learn from and apply the great things in these pages, and I also hope you will keep it in balance with the many other needs you must address as a leader in the church.

Thank you for the work you do and for the faithfulness with which you do it. If our team can ever be of help, please reach out and let me know at jimc@churchdifferencemakers.com.

Church Culture: "See It, Say It, Show It, Grow It"

Ever since the publication of Niebuhr's *Christ and Culture* in 1951, the church writ large has delved deeper and deeper into the relationship of the Christian church with the culture of the world outside of it and in which it lives. We commend this missional thrust and acknowledge that the church's purpose is to interact with the culture around it if it is to be God-honoring in impacting the lives of people. But this book is not about the culture that *surrounds* the church, it is about the culture *within* the church—your local church specifically. The discipline of church culture as a subject of research and study has flourished in recent decades, especially as the corporate world has learned ever so convincingly the role of "organizational culture" in increasing any business's efficiency, effectiveness, and profitability. Around the same time the lessons from the business world spread to countless other endeavors in virtually every realm that depends upon organizational principles to accomplish its work. In more recent times, the church world has incorporated sound business culture principles and exploded in its understanding of organizational culture behaviors to accomplish a church's mission.

This book will help make churches more effective in their mission and ministry by making their culture healthy and relevant. It is the result of conducting hundreds of workshops over the past ten years for churches and denominational judicatories on accelerating a church's growth and changing its culture. Invariably, at the end of a workshop we are asked: "This is so helpful. But do you have a book about this so I can learn more?" Well, here it is.

Church culture is more important than ever. The world is increasingly secularized. People and institutions everywhere are suffering from long-term effects of the pandemic. Social unrest and polarization have created turmoil in our country and elsewhere. These forces demand a response. Churches must be able to assess and—where needed—change their organizational culture, or they will cease to be effective or even survive. And that is to say nothing of the internal cracks and preexisting conditions in most Christian denominations, including the long season of disaffiliation within The United Methodist Church (to which most of our team members belong) and gut-wrenching stresses within other denominations and church associations. This book is written as a resource for (a) pastors of churches in denominations that are going through cataclysmic change; (b) new church-planting teams desiring to establish a healthy culture; (c) disaffiliated churches now exploring a new identity and connections; and (d) any church leaders of any tribe needing to reset their culture for any reason.

Lovett Weems says that one reason an appreciation of culture is so important is that people never make judgments about organizations, including the church, on the basis of an objective assessment of reality. People do not have enough information to make objective judgments. They make judgments based on perceptions that bear some resemblance to reality. Those perceptions are most powerfully communicated through the images of symbols and culture."[1]

In short, your church's culture—as much as and perhaps more than its worship, programs, mission outreach, and community presence—is a major force in getting new people to check it out, attend, participate, and become a disciple of Jesus Christ. The book is essentially a course, laid out to teach what I (Jim Ozier) have learned in a fifty-year ministry career pastoring churches of all sizes and in vastly different settings, and what my colleague, Yvette Thibodeaux, has learned coaching and consulting with a multitude of churches and businesses. Specifically, this book teaches the importance of assessing a local church's culture and how to implement the highly effective model of culture change. It's a process we call the "See It, Say It, Show It,

Grow It" model of creating church culture. Each part of this book takes you deeper into the importance of church culture.

Part 1, Church Culture: Understanding It and Assessing It, provides an explanation and application of church culture, including a recent history of popular research and writing about the importance of church culture for your ministry.

Understanding: "Culture eats strategy for breakfast" goes the popular quote often attributed to Peter Drucker. In the sports world, new coaches often say at their introductory press conferences, "The first thing we need to do is change the culture." It's the same in business when a new CEO is introduced: "First, we have to change the culture." Whether it is wholesale changes, targeted shifting of needed elements, or better messaging the existing culture, the importance of culture should not be denied, overlooked, or avoided. For whatever reason, other denominations and nondenominational churches have focused more on church culture than has mainline churches, like the UMC. But, in the post-pandemic church world, a church's culture is more important than ever because the long-established pre-pandemic culture of every church and organization has been shaken to the foundations. A new culture will emerge. The question is, will it be guided and led or simply random and happenchance?

Assessing: We also provide the principles of assessing a church's culture and then tools to lead a thorough assessment of your church's culture. We demonstrate how to use these tools effectively. The tools are both qualitative (observation-type interview questions) and quantitative (survey and research instruments). Tools will range from easiest to use for smaller or less complex churches to much more detailed and statistical for larger churches with multiple layers of structure.

Part 2 builds upon the emerging understanding of why to prioritize church culture in your ministry. After you have assessed your church's culture, we show how to create the culture you want in your church. How? By teaching an intentional culture-change process that works in any church of any size, the "See It, Say It, Show It, Grow It" process. Often churches and pastors fall into the temptation of assuming a church's culture is "the sum total of all the things it does." And consequently, changing the culture simply means changing the "things" the church does. However, this assumption is incorrect. We approach a church's culture not as the sum total of all the things you do, but as "the launch pad for everything you do." And we will show step by step not only the "how to's" but also the "why to's" and "when to's" that can make positive culture change a reality in your congregation! The top priority of any leader is creating and maintaining the church's culture; it is a strategic decision designed to get the results you want.

This process begins with "seeing it," which promotes an easy-to-implement methodology of the lead pastor **discovering her or his own "culture words"** and then strategically messaging them throughout the congregation to lay the foundation for the church's culture.

We continue to detail the sequential steps of the culture change/creation process and demonstrate the best places and ways to successfully (a) thread, (b) spread, and (c) embed the desired culture throughout the church to get the results you want to achieve ministry improvement and fruitful action. It doesn't help to know the laws of church culture or to have learned the lessons of creating culture if we are not able to produce results. That can only happen with congregation-wide buy-in.

Throughout the book and in the accompanying online resources, you will find easy-to-use tools in the form of graphs, charts, and visuals that can aid any pastor in teaching a congregation about navigating church culture and implementing the lessons that will help achieve that buy-in to the importance of making your church's culture your top priority.

Part 3 demonstrates how to build your "culture team" and highlights the two critical functions of this team: (a) promoting and (b) protecting the church's culture. In addition, we launch readers into the world of first-time guests and how this culture team works with the senior pastor to promote the church's culture in a way that is compelling and connects with the guests while showing how they "fit" into the church's life. The hope is that every first-time guest will walk away from their experience with your church saying to themselves, "These are the kind of people I can hang out with." That is the relational lynchpin that brings about church growth and is made possible through a clear and compelling culture.

We include two additional resources, The Complete Culture Audit and Eleven Laws of Church Culture, online at www.abingdonpress.com /culture-extras. These are powerful tools for your church's culture work and are free downloads for you to share with your leaders.

We conclude this short course by reminding readers that while church members are vitally interested in the "what" their church is doing, an unchurched first-time guest is much more interested in the "why" behind the "what." Throughout this book, we will emphasize how important it is to include the "why" behind every "what" the church is doing, which is integral to a healthy church culture.

Accordingly, this course begins with why you will benefit from reading another book on church culture.

Church Culture: Understanding It and Assessing It

Chapter 1

Why Another Book on Church Culture?

The culture of your church will reflect the values of your team.
—Tony Morgan, *The Unstuck Church*

Why is it that we are not where we should be as a church? Have you ever asked that or some similar question? Yvette and I hear it in almost every church we work in. And after ten years of reasearch, consultations, and coaching, I think we can safely say: The answer is your culture. That's why noted church author Samuel Chand—along with most other church thought leaders—maintains that "the strongest force in an organization is not vision or strategy—it is the culture which holds all the other components."[1]

Why another book on church culture? Because all churches have been somewhat shattered coming back from the pandemic, dealing with an increasingly secular world, and being caught up in the social polarization that has affected all of American society. Every church has seen its culture tested. What is church culture? And why is it so important? Chand says it forcefully, "Culture is the atmosphere in which the church functions. It is the prevalent attitude. It is the collage of spoken and unspoken messages." Every group of people has its organizational culture, including your local church.

Pastor of a fast-growing church in Texas, Stephen Blandino more recently wrote "Every organization has a unique culture, but not every organization created their culture on purpose. Most drifted into their culture.

3

Unfortunately, the same is true of churches. Culture is simply the by-product of 'the way we do things'. When you don't think strategically about what you do, the by-product is usually a mediocre—or even toxic—culture."[2] Throughout this book we'll see that culture is important, because even though it shifts over time, it also shapes the identity of the church, which impacts the strategies, mission, and ministry of the congregation. And, as every pastor knows, it is difficult to change. In the chapters that follow you will see how to lead and manage those culture shifts and changes in ways that generate goodwill and cooperation within the church.

Jenni Caldron of the 4Sight Group, which specializes in creating a great workplace culture, explains it this way: "Culture is the lynchpin connecting strategy to vision." Or as she further summarizes, "Culture is the vehicle that brings vision to life."[3]

Heather Zemple, nationally known speaker on volunteer engagement, in a presentation titled "Creating a Discipleship Culture," says it simply: "Church culture is the way most people act most of the time."[4]

Edgar Schein is generally regarded as the Father of Organizational Culture. His groundbreaking research and writing on the topic has proven foundational for further study of any organization's culture, be it corporate, educational, government, nonprofits, or even churches. If you really want to get nerdy, you can read more about him and other thought leaders on church and organizational culture in the afterword section of this book.

In his classic *Organizational Culture and Leadership*, Schein aptly points out that every organization (including in the church world) is greatly influenced by and must exist within the "macroculture." Figuratively speaking, the macroculture is the world in which we live, and of late it has drawn us all into a shattering polarization marked by distrust, disinformation, suspicion, and an almost toxic fraying of relationships, both in international events and within our own respective social communities.[5]

The macroculture has also withered under the oppressive burden of the pandemic and its aftereffects, causing almost all organizations (including churches) to see themselves as "restarts."[6]

Why another book on church culture? Because this one is written from the *perspective of and context* of a "Connectional" Church, like the UMC.

And let's face it: there is a difference between independent churches and connectional churches. There are dozens, if not hundreds, of books on church culture, but most are written from the perspective of and for the independent, stand-alone church. But as good and helpful as these books can be (I've referred to some in this manuscript), they simply do not address the "baked in" dimensions of connectional churches. So when church consultants and authors in the independent church world like Sam Chand say "To create a new culture, you must destroy the old one,"[7] this can only be said from the perspective of an independent church.

There are elements of church culture, attitudes, beliefs, and practices that are simply "baked in" and unique to connectional churches: for connectional churches (like the UMC) each local church is intricately intertwined and connected to every other church and to the larger denominational body. Thus, "destroying the culture" is not a simple or necessarily desirable thing. The "baked in" elements keep each church connected to the larger denomination. These include things like pastoral appointments, acquiring and dismissing staff members, and budgeting—as well as hundreds of years of shared experience with connected values, practices, and expectations.

While we believe any and every church can benefit from the tools and techniques and substance of this book, it is written specifically with connectional churches in mind.

The Importance of This Book

As a lay person, I (Yvette) have been asking the same question that opens this part of our book since before I began consulting with churches: *"Why is it that we are not where I know we should be as a church?"*

As corporations, communities, governments, and churches seek to establish an identity that connects with people and the world, they are recognizing that it starts with defining their culture. It starts with building and effectively managing and messaging your culture so that you can live into your purpose, achieve your goals, fulfill your desired results, and maintain a relevancy and connection to those around you, wherever you are located and to whatever community culture God is calling you to reach. Corporations are now judged by their culture, not just the quality of the products and services they provide. For example, Chick-fil-A is known for their corporate culture as well as the cows used in their advertising. Verizon Wireless, for whom I worked nineteen years, established an amazing culture built upon the desire of providing the best network to gain prominence in the wireless industry.

The church itself, knowingly or unknowingly, is marketed and judged for its culture. Therefore, whether you are a church planter, a transitioning pastor, or a long-tenured pastor, you must understand the importance of culture and the need to **see it, say it, show it, grow it** if you want to fully achieve impactful mission and vision, no matter your church's setting.

I don't know if God had culture in mind, but thank God that he sent his son Jesus to the world. Jesus came because the world's culture was overtaking God's desired results for humankind and his creation, as he had established through the old covenant. But times changed and God saw the promise of entering into a new covenant, which would birth a new culture, so the church could change the world. Out of this new covenant, the church was established, and in his departing, Jesus, in Matthew 28:19-20, gave the church a commandment: "Therefore, go and make disciples of all nations, baptizing them in the name of the Father and of the Son and of the Holy Spirit, teaching them to obey everything that I've commanded you. Look, I myself will be with you every day until the end of this present age" (CEB). This is what the community of faith does; culture is how it goes about doing what it does in every setting and situation under the sun. In other words, Jesus told the church to go out into the world and become the ultimate influencer for Christ. He admonished us that if we get the "how" right, the rest is up to him. We do this by being intentional about the culture we establish. And we establish culture when we **see it, say it, show it, grow it.**

Your local church is a microculture within the macroculture of (a) its denomination (or nondenominational church network), (b) the community where it is located, and (3) the general social world all around it. That is why the underlying church culture of a United Methodist congregation may be different from the underlying culture of a nondenominational church. Among other considerations, the "microculture" operates within the "macroculture," and it is impossible to truly understand one without the other. Interestingly, as we will also detail throughout the book, each local church is made up of a number of smaller internal microcultures. In that understanding, your local church becomes a macroculture made up of a number of smaller microcultures. For instance, a healthy church culture will foster Sunday school classes whose culture may be a bit different—allowing for the "identity" of a particular class—but should mirror the culture of the church as a whole. Troubles arise when a church's microcultures begin to be inconsistent with or even contradictory to the larger macroculture. Usually when this happens, the church's culture stagnates or even becomes toxic.

Organizational church culture is not confined to academic, social study. Jesus himself created a culture through the Holy Spirit in which followers could connect in community and thrive: "I give you a new commandment, that you love one another," he said in John 13:34 (NRSVUE). It must have worked because Tertullian, the ancient church historian, later remarked, "See how they love each other." We will see in Part 2 how Jesus taught in the Beatitudes and modeled in the washing of his disciples' feet this culture around which the whole Christian movement is centered.

John Wesley and creating culture: Great religious movements and their leaders displayed the power of creating a strong culture. Historians generally agree that John Wesley was instrumental in changing the culture of America. But before he could change the outside culture, he had to create an internal culture that we have come to know as the Methodist Movement. Remember, culture is "how we go about doing the things we do." Wesley made famous a movement built on "social holiness" through small groups and discipleship groups and with an intentional focus of adherents growing in faith by being together. A visionary, "whose heart was strangely warmed," created a culture that came to life through systems of growing followers and turning them into disciples. Had he left journals and sermons and letters instructing people just "what to do" that would have become transitory legalism and not likely to last multiple generations; had his methodology (ridiculed as "methodists") ended with "how to do it," that would have been dogmatic. But his legacy reveals a lot of "how to go about doing what we do," and that is fundamental to his creating a culture that has had lasting effects for generations. You can see the intentionality of this in what has become known as Wesley's three simple rules: (1) Do no harm; (2) Do good; and (3) Stay in love with God.[8]

His further writings indicate an intentionality of culture creation:

- *"Light yourself on fire with passion and people will come from miles to watch you burn."*

- *"Earn all you can, give all you can, save all you can."*

- *"Though we cannot think alike, may we not love alike? May we not be of one heart, though we are not of one opinion? Without all doubt, we may."*

- *"Though I am always in haste, I am never in a hurry."*

The now-famous quote, "Do all the good you can, by all the means you can, in all the ways you can, in all the places you can, at all the times you can, to all the people you can, as long as ever you can," has traditionally been attributed to Wesley. More recent historical research deems the quote is not found in his writings.[9] But there is no question the sentiment found within it has been held dear for generations of followers and has been instrumental in growing the culture of the Methodist movement.

What makes your church compelling? What draws people to it? What features, challenges, and opportunities make it pop and sizzle with excitement? What would you like them to be? Churches often mistakenly assume that their culture is the "sum total of all the things they do," However, the "little things" or even the "big things" that a church does—or changes—to achieve desired results seldom produce the hoped-for fruits. Yvette's experience working with a church who did a "big thing" in hopes of creating a big change fleshes this principle out in tangible ways.

A church with which I (Yvette) consulted (out of courtesy I will not mention its real name but will refer to it as the Church of All People in this and the next few illustrations) recognized that the community around them was changing and their members were either aging out or moving away. They went into survival mode and decided they needed to become more diverse to maintain membership. They initially thought that if they just brought in an African American pastor and gave him leadership over a contemporary service that African Americans in the surrounding area would start attending. What they quickly observed is that merely adding an African American pastor did not translate into having a culture that was inviting to African Americans in the community. After many conversations, I encouraged the church to take an honest look at their culture. What was missing in making a connection with the community was the "how" and "why"; they had a culture issue. Remember, culture is tied to passion and emotions, and especially in the church, it is vested in the heart. This church needed to do a deep cultural assessment—"a look at the heart." Shifts in the ethnic makeup of a church typically mean a shift in culture. There has to be a willingness to let go of some comforts to make more people comfortable. There can be honoring the past and embracing a new and different future. A church can evolve their culture without losing their past. Finally, just like this church observed, a failure to evolve often means stagnant numbers and slow death for a church; especially if the existing culture no longer supports your mission and vision.

Focusing on "changing things" rather than "changing culture" often leads to chasing rabbits, and soon it becomes directionless. Instead of be-lieving the false assumption that "the church's culture is the sum total of all the things you do," understand that "a healthy culture becomes the launch-pad for everything you do." If you hold to the former approach, you cling to the faulty idea that to change your culture, you change the things you do. Actually, it is just the opposite: changing the culture will change things, or at least sharpen them and align them for more fruitful results. Change the culture and that will change the church! And it can grow the church! Change the culture and grow the church! In Part 2 we'll look step by step at how to do that.

Chapter 2

Church Culture: What It Is and What It Isn't

Culture is usually unnoticed, unspoken, and unexamined.
—Samuel R.Chand, *Cracking Your Church's Culture Code*

I t is commonly understood in the church world that culture is important because it shapes the way things are done in any local church.
Strategies easily come and go, but culture is deeply embedded and difficult to change. As Lovett Weems says,

> Webster defines the word culture as, "the integrated pattern of human be-
> havior that includes that includes thought, speech, action and artifacts."
> Families, organizations and entire nations possess cultures. Culture repre-
> sents "the way we do things around here"; it is how we behave most of the
> time.[1]

Or, as he adds, quoting Denham Grierson from *Transforming a People
of God*, "At a deeper and less visible level, culture represents the values that
are shared by the people in a group and tend to persist over time, even when
the group membership changes."[2]

So, as we are discussing what church culture *is*, let's take a look what
church culture is *not*. It is *not* your mission statement (which clearly and
concisely trumpets your purpose); it is not your vision statement (which
succinctly sets your direction). While both are crucial in your church's leadership work and we highly recommend these be clearly articulated within
your congregation, they are not your church's culture. Your mission and vision help differentiate you from other churches and provide a bit of identity

for church members to rally around and a function to motivate. But purpose, direction, and function do not paint a picture of your church's culture. They are about what a church *does*.

Church culture is *not* "what you do" in your ministry. It is *how* you go about doing what you do. And it messages to the "why" behind the "what" you do. For the church, culture tells a story that resonates with the heart and passions of the people you seek to reach. Church culture has the potential to make an emotional and spiritual connection to what people believe and desire to see present in their church. It offers an explanation for why people from all walks of life come together every Sunday, serve in the ministries of the church, and volunteer their time and talents, and give generously to the mission.

Take communion for example. It is a "what" that most churches do. It is a special time, a sacred moment, a ritual of bonding and obedience. Most communion instructions by the pastor or officiant will include the biblical "why" ("This is not our table; it is the Lord's. All are welcome who have a sincere desire to be closer to God," etc.). The "how" may be by intinction or common cup or passing the elements through the pews or congregants kneeling at the rail to receive the elements. And so on.

But it is the "how we go about doing what we do" in which the culture of the church is messaged and communicated. I (Jim) and our worship team at Trietsch Memorial United Methodist Church, which I served as long-tenured pastor, remained intentional about creating a culture of closeness, personalness, and being relational. I shared with the participants that as pastor I would bless the elements as is the custom of the church. And then I further informed the congregation that staff members and volunteers would serve each person one by one as I moved around the platform blessing participants, praying for them if I happen to know of a personal need or simply if I felt led by God. I touched the hands of all the youth, saying, "God has great need of you." Can you just feel the relational culture exuding to all through that intentional messaging?

As well, I gave these instructions: "When you approach the communion rail, we invite you to fold your hands and extend them across the rail. If you would like me to pray for you personally, you please say your first name when the server arrives as a way of presenting your whole self to Christ at this sacred moment." (Notice this practice also allows the server to hear the person's name and then to repeat it: "Sharon, this is the love of Christ given for you and for the world.") See how it becomes ultra personal? There may be multiple variations of this same type of process. The important point is that it was not the practice but the culture messaging that was most important!

After eighteen years I moved to a different assignment, and my successor wanted to do communion with a few tweaks. No problem! A healthy culture allows for flexibility and change because the bedrock values have already been planted. Thirty years later, through subsequent pastors, the culture practice remains.

Even AI gets it. Culture is important! A Google search of organizational culture reveals this AI description: "Organizational culture is sometimes called the glue that holds an organization together. It is the silent code of conduct that's more about how things get done than what gets done here. It can also be called 'white noise' which is background static that may affect you, but goes unnoticed."

While we provide lengthy background material on the academic understanding of organizational culture in our afterword section, most experts who study organizational culture agree that it is simply "how we do things around here."[3]

Church Culture: Your Top Priority

The culture of your church determines who comes and who stays.
—Kevin Gerald, *By Design or Default*

There are myriad ways of talking about, thinking about, and acting upon something so important as church culture. That is probably because the very topic is both evident and yet elusive to define and describe.[1]

Regardless of the nuances, culture should be every church's top priority. Especially now, when many churches are struggling with self-identity and outward expressions of their ministry. The church (the church at large and your local church) is reeling under the pressure of many conflicting and disrupting forces that threaten the health of the institution. Just like in the human body, our internal health suffers under external duress. No church is immune from the prevailing counter-winds in this season. And as so often happens, when the church feels forced to attend to its own survival, care for its culture is relegated to a back-burner issue, which only compounds the problem.

Within our tribe (Jim Ozier, Yvette Thibodaux, and Jim Chandler), The United Methodist Church continues to struggle through the splintering of our denomination over sexuality and biblical exegesis issues. This splintering has already led to the formation of at least one new traditional denomination (The Global Methodist Church), plus a growing network of former UMC churches like the one led by the Orchard Church and probably other offshoots.

I imagine that right now without reading another word, you can capture a good sense of what your church's culture is. It is best not to talk about a "good" or "bad" culture but a "healthy" or "unhealthy" culture. As Patrick Lencioni observes, "The health of an organization is the single greatest factor determining its success."[2] Is your church a caring, positive, vital outpost for God? Is it a fun place to be? Is it a rewarding experience? Can you just *not* stop talking about it! That's good health and comes from and contributes to a great culture.

Outside forces (macroculture) like social polarization, political upheaval, and global fragility have punctured a hole into the very fabric of what we thought the world was and would forever be. How do you respond to those forces?

Internal forces (within the macroculture) are just as powerful. If a church is exploring disaffiliating with the intent to become independent, or to re-affiliate with some other group, the church will be affected in unforeseen ways by the church's new macroculture. So, churches considering disaffiliation that might intentionally go somewhere else beyond the UMC are advised to expand their search criteria beyond theological, but to look at cultural affinity. Be intentional!

Many churches are facing culture shifts (intentional or managed change), but even more are going through culture drift (unintentional and directionless); let's hope it does not become culture rifts that tear apart and dishonor the gospel.

We hope that in reading this, leaders will be convinced that their number-one responsibility is to assess, create, maintain, and protect the culture of their church. And there is yet another reason that this book on church culture is so timely for today: because of all the pressures from the general church world, from denominational splintering, and from the erosion of social norms in the world at large that so profoundly affect the local church.

This book has been ten years in the making, but it is especially important to publish now. Why? Because in the UMC tribe, the rush is on—the rush to respond to the disaffiliation season faithfully and positively with an observable sense of urgency, to take advantage of the moment. It is with a good heart and a determined commitment that many conferences are rushing to find appropriate ways to respond. And one of those ways is to start new UMC congregations, frequently made up of a core group of people who wished to remain UMC but whose churches voted to disaffiliate. We commend and encourage this effort, and at the same time we lift up necessary cautions.

Frequently these new churches are birthed or planted in the traditional model of developing a committed core group, but with a new twist. That core group may well be made up of people (sometimes referred to as refugees) from two or three or more nearby churches that have voted to disaffiliate from the UMC. We anticipate that these new churches are getting started with an adrenaline rush. But when that adrenaline rush wears off, the new church will need to face head-on the challenge of blending multiple church cultures together to sustain vitality for the long term.

There will be many "that's not the way we did it at our church" and similar sentiments. There may surface other hidden obstacles that can certainly be overcome, but only with intentionality on the part of the pastor and key leaders. So don't rush into this adventure; take your time, digest it, and process it with friends and team members.

Within The United Methodist Church, around six thousand churches and clergy have chosen to disaffiliate, and many are exploring becoming part of some other already-existing denominational connection or some entirely new one just being birthed into existence. And those choosing to remain United Methodist will be tasked with developing a new culture to meet a new church world.

It is understandable that these churches and pastors choosing the path of disaffiliation often make the theological and social alignment of any possible future connection the main focus of their discernment for where they will go next. But they need to be sure that there is a good cultural match as well. The urgent and seemingly never-ending radical shifts within the larger macroculture of our world demand that every local church take a fresh look at its organizational culture, and that's what this book enables you to do. And more.

This is a book about assessing your church's culture and then discerning if it needs to be (a) strengthened, (b) changed, or (c) simply better messaged. Assessing a church's culture and learning how to be more adept at assessing the culture of other organizations will be essential for those churches remaining within the UMC as the denomination readjusts in response to the painful splintering. It is equally critical for individual churches, should they decide to become independent or join some other denomination, because if the culture fit isn't there, it will lead to even greater challenges down the road.

You need not feel stuck with the current culture of your church, but you must honor it and where it came from and how it got to be the culture of your church. As Dr. Roy Spore notes, "Every Local Church has its own unique culture, derived from years and decades of the people living together, working together, suffering together, and rejoicing together."[3]

And it is also true that the church's culture, which may have been years in the making, has also over time lost its relevancy or become static or even toxic. As you will see in Part 2, you can change it. But you can't just make up the culture you want out of fantasy land; rather you create it or discover it out of a variety of tendencies, based on your priorities and the results you need to see in and from your church.

In your church you no doubt have people with different viewpoints on a whole host of issues: politics, theology, ministry practices, and church direction. A great culture can overcome these differences, and there are many other necessary benefits, as you can see from figure 1.

As with all of life, we make our choices, and our choices make us. You will see throughout this book, the choices a church makes (a) reveals its identity, (b) creates its culture, and (c) determines the results it achieves in whatever it determines to be its mission/ministry measurables.

BENEFITS OF A GREAT CHURCH CULTURE

"When we respond to what circumstances are put upon us, with what God put within us, then we can transform the world around us."

A healthy church **CULTURE** is a difference maker for your church when it is:

C
U
L
T
U
R
E

CREATIVELY
UNLEASHING
LOVE
TRUST
UNITY
RESPECT
EXCITEMENT

A great church culture brings **PEACE** to your church when it is:

P
E
A
C
E

POSITIVE
ENGAGING
ACCEPTING
COMPELLING
ENCOURAGING

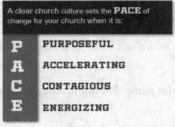

A clear church culture sets the **PACE** of change for your church when it is:

P
A
C
E

PURPOSEFUL
ACCELERATING
CONTAGIOUS
ENERGIZING

"I give you a new commandment, that you love one another." John 13:34

"See how they love each other."
Tertullian, ancient historian commenting on Jesus's followers

D FFERENCE
MAKERS

In our workshops on church culture, we often share the following funny tidbit. When I (Ozier) was pastoring a large church in North Texas, our men's fellowship group took an incredible fishing trip for peacock bass in the Amazon River basin. In preparation, one of the men found this on-line and shared it with us:

What to do if you are attacked by an anaconda

The following is from the Peace Corps Manual for its volunteers working in the Amazon River Basin to respond to a possible encounter with an Anaconda.

Number 1: If you are attacked by an anaconda, do not run. The snake is faster than you are.

Number 2: Lie flat on the ground. Put your arms tight against your side, your legs tight against one another.

Number 3: Tuck your chin in.

Number 4: The snake will come and begin to nudge and climb over your body.

Number 5: Do not panic. I'm not making this up. This is what it really says!

Number 6: After the snake has examined you, it will begin to swallow you from the feet and always from the end. Permit the snake to swallow your feet and ankles. Do not panic.

Number 7: The snake will now begin to suck your legs into its body. You must lie perfectly still. This will take a long time. I'm not making this up.

Number 8: When the snake has reached your knees, slowly and with as little as movement as possible reach down, take your knife and very gently slide it into the side of the snake's mouth between the edge of its mouth and your leg then suddenly rip upwards severing the snake's head.

Number 9: Be sure you have your knife!

Of course, the crowds erupt in laughter at the obvious irony in this, as we explain, "Now I don't know about you, but I think that should have been a little higher up on the list!" And number 10 is equally important: "Make sure your knife is sharp!"

It doesn't take long before a pastor in ministry realizes that much of church life is like that anaconda. Sunday after Sunday after Sunday after Sunday comes at you fast. Problem after problem after problem pursues us relentlessly. COVID-19, denominational uncertainty, social turmoil, polarized congregants, and lack of direction have squeezed the life joy of ministry right out of many clergy and church leaders.

Let us say it emphatically: your culture is your knife! And this short course will help keep it sharp. It is what allows you to cut through the clutter of distractions, to slice through the competing and often contradictory demands on your time. Your culture allows you to carve out the ministry results you want to have and feel called to fulfill.

But all too often, like the knife in the anaconda story, we prioritize church culture way too low; and when we truly, really, desperately need it, it is too late. Hopefully, we all agree by now that our church's culture is our top priority. And we hope this book and other training resources help keep your knife sharp. But before we move to ways to assess your church's culture, please read the next chapter on a circumstance needing special attention when it comes to church culture: church planting. Now, most readers will not be church planters, but we think you'll see that the principles in this next chapter can apply to almost any existing church.

Chapter 4

Planting Culture in a New Church Start

The Culture Equation:
Relationships+vision+systems+accountability+leadership=Culture
—Stephen Bandino, *Creating Your Church's Culture*

Much of our discussion has focused on changing a church's culture to meet the challenges of changing times. But what about church planting when the emphasis is more on creating a new culture rather than changing an existing one?

Church planting today must take account of starting something new in a splintered church, a polarized population, and a world rebounding from COVID-19 and social upheaval.

A "boll weevil moment" is in front of new church planters. In Enterprise, Alabama, is the intriguing Boll Weevil Monument, erected by local residents for a dramatic reason. Years ago, in that part of Alabama, the boll weevil came and destroyed the cotton crop, the mainstay of the area economy. With the cotton crop lost year after year, the town suffered: schools closed, churches shuttered, businesses disappeared, and people moved away. But the remnant—with coaching and consultation from agronomists—learned how to plant new crops that didn't treacherously drain the soil of so many nutrients and that were not subject to the boll weevil's appetite. Within a few years Enterprise became more prosperous than ever. So they erected the monument "hailing the beetle as a herald of prosperity" because what they thought was the worst thing that could ever happen turned out to be the best thing that ever happened to the town and its economy.

Planters, you are the monument in this day and age. Many people, including churchgoers, have felt victimized by the pandemic, by denominational splintering, by social upheaval and polarization, and by the general decline in influence of religion, Christianity, and the local church.

But we are all learning that what we thought was the worst thing that could ever happen may turn out to be the best thing that ever happened! All throughout the church world we are forced to learn to do and be the church in different and new ways that we could barely have imagined just a few years ago.

Planters have the opportunity to lead a boll weevil moment at this time in church history! In this chapter we will share some keys to create such a moment in spite of—and perhaps because of—this crazy world into which you are planting. For simplicity's sake, we call these keys the new ABCs to creating a boll weevil moment:

- Approach
- Brand
- Culture

Approach

There are many approaches to planting, and hopefully the approach taken for a new church start will have been arrived at through a thorough assessment of the setting, demographics, and desired results for the new church coming into being. Some new church starts will be more or less the "traditional" approach, which in itself has a number of expressions.

The new church start may be a "parachute drop" in which a gifted planter selected by the denomination or a church-planting network is "dropped" with considerable seed money but no evident connection into a demographically ripe neighborhood. It may be a "mother-daughter extension campus" spinning off from a healthy existing congregation. Or it may be what is sometimes referred to as an "unplanned pregnancy," which is when a subgroup splits off from its mother church for reasons good or bad. Of course, the approach of your new church start may be some kind of fresh expression with a nontraditional model like a coffee shop, diner, bar, or something else totally new! You may be planting a viral church based on social media and digital outreach; God may have put in your heart something totally new, awaiting your creative energy; you may be planting a new church start made up of a core group of folk from one or more UMC churches who wish to remain UMC after their home churches have voted to disaffiliate. Path1, the church planting and multiplication movement of the UMC provides deeper insights into these approaches, as do planting movements started by some other denominational or church-planting network. Regardless of the approach, it must be intentional and take into account the fierce pressures of our current, secularized world. This changing world is certainly evidence that new churches and faith communities are needed!

But whatever the approach, more than likely it will hinge on at least three dynamics. The first dynamic is assessing the setting, community, and needs to be met. Second is assembling a group of like-minded people, from which you can develop a launch team to help start the new church. The group of like-minded people may include close friends, people from the neighborhood, members of nearby supportive churches, or refugees from churches that have voted to disaffiliate. But from that group, only the planter's discernment, training, and motivation can create the launch team. In our tribe, every conference has a congregational developer who can help in shaping the launch team. Regardless of its size (it will vary depending upon circumstances) and makeup (when, how, and why it meets), the launch team will become the soil into which a wise planter plants the seeds of the new church's culture. So read carefully the sections of this book on creating culture.

There is a truism often recited by those responsible for starting new churches: "Every launch team starts with a group of people, but not every group of people becomes a launch team." That is, you may assemble a group of people with an interest in starting a new church, but that group may not actually have the commitment to become a launch team. Thank God for "interested people"; don't disparage them. But take care not to assume that showing interest in a launch team translates into joining a launch team. One of the benefits of beginning to create your culture intentionally and early, is that the culture itself will help some people drop out of your launch team and others enthusiastically want to join the team! Creating a healthy church culture is never-ending, but it must have a beginning. So early on, be prepared (as this book will enable you to be) to plant the seeds of culture and to begin the process of creating the culture of your new church, regardless of the approach the church plant will take.

The third dynamic required to make any new church-planting approach work is the planter and launch team members having the attitude that "we are not victims"—that is, having the attitude of an overcomer, in which a positive nature, a resilient mindset, and a "yes, we can" spirit are authentically and abundantly evidenced. Planting the culture early on into the launch team intentionally allows for an environment of prayer, support, and genuine love. Whatever your approach, wouldn't you agree that this is the kind of attitude you want to bring into the birthing?

Brand

New churches being planted in this season of church life are doing so when the "brand" of any church and all churches is somewhat shaken. What planters are embarking upon is being done in rather risky times, because the brand of religion in general is not so positive.

Jake Meador probes the reasons that the brand of Christianity (and all religions in America) seems to be diminishing in recent times in a *Washington Post* article titled "The Misunderstood Reason Millions Stopped Going to Church." Surprisingly, one of the main reasons he lifts up is simply the way American life is wired to be right now: "workism" and tight schedules that tend to squeeze organized church participation out of our busy routines.[1] But for me, the powerful impact of his article wasn't the technical "macro" understanding of the research and trends and numbers. It was his personalizing the findings into his own life:

23

Forty million Americans have stopped attending church in the past 25 years. That's something like 12 percent of the population, and it represents the largest concentrated change in church attendance in American history. As a Christian, I feel this shift acutely. My wife and I wonder whether the institutions and communities that have helped preserve us in our own faith will still exist for our four children, let alone whatever grandkids we might one day have.[2]

Adding to the diminishing influence of all religions, Christian denominations such as the Roman Catholic Church, the UMC, Baptists, and so on (and well-known independent megachurches) are often tagged with media stories of corruption by church leaders, clergy sex-abuse scandals, and chaotic internal struggles of theology, biblical interpretation, and structure. The result is that the wider brand of religion, and even Christianity, is tainted and bruised, contributing to the perceptible decline in influence of mainline denominations and creating frustration, apathy, and disinterest.

There is good news! Church planters are in a position to help "rehabilitate" the brand, not only of your particular tribe, but of Christianity as well! Your brand is not only used for marketing (although for marketing it is essential); it is also for your identity; it builds the connectional bridges that allow adherents to keep on mission and can open doors for new people to become part of the community of Jesus Christ for the first time!

But it is also a reality that the brand of any new church may well be viewed with renewed scrutiny by an ever-increasingly skeptical population. In our tribe (the UMC), for instance, we acknowledge that our denomination is a splintered by disaffiliations; but also our brand has been shattered. Here's why:

a. **Bad publicity.** In many conferences, legal fights have resulted in negative publicity within local communities and among the denominational perception at large.

b. **Targeting.** Much like during the American Civil War, friends have been pitted against friends; families who worshipped together for generations have seen their allegiances and community torn apart. Faithful church members often report that they feel targeted for criticism and in some cases even ridicule. In such an environment, it is easy to become

24

negative, aggressive, and even spiteful toward others who see our denominational issues differently. These attitudes and actions can easily spill over from the church itself into the community. Other churches can unintentionally or intentionally recruit against the whole Methodist brand.

c. **Influence.** National polls measuring the influence of religion as a force in American society show a steady decline. Even aside from internal negative issues, it is harder to plant a new church when there is less demand for what the church has to offer. Adding to declining influence in general, our internal squabbles, of which negative perceptions have spread beyond the church into the community, and you can see the shattering of our brand.

d. **Overt and covert competition.** It is no longer rare to see stories of disgruntled church members distraught over their church's vote to not disaffiliate following a popular staff person who personally left the UMC to start a new competing church just down the street, often with a brand name closely similar to their beloved church, and frequently recruiting church members from the established church to the new start-up.

Even taking all of the above into account, the planter is responsible for developing the "brand" of the new church, and to do it quickly. Tony Jeary, one of the nation's leading coaches whose clients include many Fortune 500 organizations, stresses the importance of brand: "We all have a brand. Top leaders are strategic about building theirs."[3]

Culture

When we speak of culture, we recognize that every church operates within at least three cultures: the culture of the surrounding community, the culture of the denomination or church network, and the organizational culture of the local church itself. While the three cannot be separated, this book focuses its attention to the local church's organizational culture.

In the preceding and following pages you will have learned a lot about church culture. In this section our purpose is to remind planters that planting a church today will require much more attention to creating the culture of the church. Four ingredients bring a church's culture into focus: (1) Leadership and values; (2) Vision Statement; (3) Symbols, ceremonies, and celebrations (the things you honor, remember, and cheer for are the things you value most); (4) You as the Leader.[4]

Changing your church's culture will probably not be applicable, because in most cases there is not existing culture to assess or change. It is all new! We say "in most cases" because if you are planting a church with a core leadership group made up of former members from one or more UM churches that voted to disaffiliate, you will have the delicate task of blending multiple cultures or reshapiwng the residue from previous cultures into a new one that you are planting.

Planting often brings up the image of seeds, which implies something growing. However, be cautious about what is being planted. Remember Jesus's teaching in Matthew 13:24-30 (NRSVUE) about the sower planting seeds of wheat, but during the night an enemy planted seeds of weeds. Can't you just agonize with the workers who asked their master when the weeds and wheat started to come up at the same time: "Do you want us to go pull up the weeds?" Replied the sower, "No, because in pulling up the weeds you might also pull up the wheat." Jesus ended the parable by the sower telling his workers "to let both the wheat and the weeds grow to harvest, and at harvest time I will separate the weeds from the wheat," as a parable to talk about the end-times judgment.

But our interest here is in the agony of seeing the weeds and the wheat planted together and how challenging it is to separate them. When a new church is planted, it is planted with seeds of hope and the best of intentions; but be cautious, it can also be unintentionally planted with the seeds of its own destruction.[5]

By 2014, Mars Hill Church in Seattle had grown to fifteen thousand people in fifteen locations. But before the year was over, the church collapsed. On January 1, 2015, Mars Hill was gone. Pastor Mark Driscoll was for years one of the most sought-after, popular preachers in the evangelical church world. Thousands flocked to hear him preach every week, and thousands more Christian leaders registered for conferences and workshops around the country to learn from him. For a season, he seemed to be the shining example of the best wheat growing anywhere. But almost overnight, the toxicity of the culture he planted became weeds that grew so significant it ruined the whole thing.

The value of this case study is not just the fascinating dynamics of a particularly toxic church culture a couple of decades ago, but it has many insights for church planters about the importance of planting a healthy culture into a new church start.

If you are a planter reading this book, pay close attention to what your needs may be. You may or may not need to do much assessing or changing of a culture; but the principles of creating a new culture found in these pages will remain relevant as you move forward. And as you move forward to plant your church, remember this truism: "Church culture is not the sum total of all the things you do; it is the launchpad for everything you do."

That is to say, be aware of the great temptation to plant a church based on "things." By things we mean programs, events, worship settings, and activities. Planters will receive great pressure from supervisors and constituents to "get things done." It may take a while, but eventually you'll learn that you can't "out thing" other existing churches or other new church plants. There is always some other church that has the ability, funding, and people to do most any "thing" better than you can.

"Thing"-based church plants can often start great, but it is the church's culture that allows for sustainability and viability. It is great to plant a new church but start with its culture. The good news is that you have a new opportunity; the bad news is the stakes are really high to get it right. Remember the parable Jesus told in Luke's Gospel: "Which of you, desiring to build a tower, does not first sit down and count the cost, whether he has enough to complete it? Otherwise, he will not finish it and will be ridiculed as a fool" (Luke 14:28-29 NRSVUE).

Planters, it is important to get this right. You don't want this new venture to struggle. A fiasco can be an embarrassment for years to come and further diminish the denomination's brand. Especially in a new church, its culture is your top priority. The importance of planting culture into your new church, within our tribe for instance, is the immediate pressure to get something planted. Why? Because of that unstated dynamic we highlighted in the previous chapter, that is, the adrenaline rush to get new churches started. As we mentioned in the previous chapter, there is a high-pressured adrenaline rush within the UMC fueled by three dynamics, none of which is bad, but all of which deserve a word of caution:

a. **Response.** This high-octane fuel drives denominational leaders and church members to demonstrate that we can withstand this season of disaffiliations. Even if we are losing 20 percent of our congregations, we're down but not out; we want to have a positive and demonstrable response that will hopefully create new momentum.

b. **Resources.** Because of disaffiliations and their accompanying buyouts, in many cases annual conferences are flush with newfound cash. At least in the short term, there is money to start new churches. And dollars aren't the only resource; in some cases, there may be more pastors available to serve fewer churches, which creates a healthier pool of potential planters.

c. **Refugees.** All around the country there are new churches being planted that are made up of UMC members who want to remain with the UMC, even after their beloved churches have voted to disaffiliate. In many annual conferences, those wishing to remain in the UMC have sought out other like-minded folk from other churches to come up with a positive response after disaffiliation. Sometimes they simply join a nearby UMC and benefit from what are often referred to as "lighthouse" churches who make an intentional effort to reach these refugees from disaffiliation votes. In other cases, these refugees from one or more disaffiliated churches become the core group of a new UMC church plant.

The adrenaline rush fueled by the three Rs (Response, Resources, Refugees) is an exciting and thoughtful initiative, which has already blessed countless people in countless ways. But caution! We still must count the cost and be prepared for what happens when the adrenaline rush subsides: systematic strategic planning, long-term support training, and appropriate organizational culture emphasis.

All the "things" that a new church can do (depending upon its approach and leveraging the brand in positive ways) can be well conceived and taught in various church-planting bootcamps and workshops. The things are crucial and cannot be ignored; but while things build momentum, culture creates sustainability, viability, and growth.

Over the past several decades, mainline church planting has tended to be "thing"-based, unintentionally developing an attractional model (do the right things and people will come to see and participate in the things). How do we grow? Do the next new "cool thing." With the best of intentions, we unwittingly train prospects and participants to be consumers of the church's ministry. Nondenominational new church plants have tended to be more culture'-oriented, creating a clear and compelling identity to which prospects can relate. With the best of intentions, they create a climate where people can become producers of the church's ministry.

Remember, organizational culture is not "what we do" (most churches do mostly the same things), but "how we go about doing what we do." Planting the church culture in your new church start is the most important thing you'll do. It is the attitude, the spirit, the experience, the heartbeat of congregational life. That is what unchurched prospects relate to and allows your church to grow. Even though as a planter you are not assessing a highly ingrained culture, the parts on creating culture are all the same; read carefully. And always ask about desired results: What are the desired results? Are we getting them? What's blocking them?

Planting culture in a new church can help you rehabilitate the brand; but more importantly you are planting something new to which new peo-

29

ple—perhaps people who are unchurched or dechurched for any number of reasons—can find new hope and new life! Remember that old Americana bit of wisdom: "You can count the seeds in an apple, but you can't count the apples in a seed." What you are doing will have amazing and long-lasting impact; that's why planters make a difference for Jesus Christ!

Church Governance and Structure

Whether starting a new church, restarting a changing church, or pastoring an existing church, questions about your church's governance and structure are sure to come up. Unfortunately, many times these questions become more prominent than your church's culture. Remember that a multitude of church leaders are there to promote and protect your church's *structure*. Since you are the pastor, it is your job to promote and protect the church's *culture*. This book's focus is on the culture, not the nitty-gritty of church structure. But we hear it all the time: when it comes to church structure and governance, the voiced anxiety is it is being overburdened with complexity, redundancy, and bureaucracy. Consequently, and rightfully so, the need to "restructure" is often a must. Fortunately, there are a number of helpful resources out there to help churches restructure and reset their ministry. But a word of caution: restructuring without reshaping, refining, and revisioning your church's culture can mostly result in just spinning a different set of wheels.

One additional word of caution for planters and for those hoping to reshape their church's culture: It is both tempting and easier to duplicate than to innovate! But avoid an over-dependence upon duplicating what happens to be successful and trendy in the popular church world at any given moment. Sometimes there is a need to reinvent the wheel!

As Robert Lewis and Wayne Cordeiro spell out in their book, *Culture Shift: Transforming Your Church from the Inside,*

> What's so unhealthy about duplicating or cloning another church's approach to ministry? You don't need to think creatively. Programs don't require much innovation. You are simply copying another program or leader. As church leaders merely duplicate someone else's vision, they diminish their innovative, creative, and entrepreneurial side. Their gears

become frozen; so long as they focus on copying someone else's ministry, they don't learn to get the stuck gears going.[6]

Once church leadership decides to make its culture a priority, then it can take the next steps: (1) assessing the current culture; (2) discerning if what is needed is to make targeted tweaks to an already healthy culture; (3) learning how to make significant culture shifts; and (4) if need be, setting in motion a congregation-wide strategic process of wholesale culture change.

Principles of Assessing Church Culture

Regardless of where your church falls on the culture continuum, your church's culture can improve; you can uproot mediocrity and create a healthy vibrant culture.
—Marcus Carlson, *Habits of Healthy Churches*

Longtime acclaimed church consultant Aubrey Malphurs, in his book *Look Before You Lead*, offers insights into culture using the metaphor of an apple: "Its skin is the church's outward behavior; its flesh is the church's values; its core is the church's beliefs."[1] When you set out to assess your church's culture, you are biting into all three: its behaviors, beliefs, and values. And the congregation is built around allegiance to all three. That's why most congregants jealously cling to their current culture. So progress carefully and respectfully as you assess.

There are five leading principles that any organization can use when assessing its culture. They provide a set of tools that can be used to gain objective insights about the current culture of an organization, a community, and even your own church. The five leading principles to assessing your church's culture are:

- Hallowed ground
- Healthy/unhealthy
- Desired results

- Intentional
- Ask

Hallowed Ground

As Jim Chandler shared in the foreword, assessing your church's culture is a journey through hallowed ground. Your church's culture is not something abstract; it is contextualized in the church's history. If your church has been around for any time at all, it exists because people over the years have loved it. Countless people have sacrificed time, talents, and treasure to build the church.

People have laughed at the preacher's jokes, wept at weddings, cheered at baptisms, sobbed at funerals, been married and buried, and made friendships that have lasted a lifetime. The church is where their children were raised, where they learned the values that have shaped their lives ever since. In short, the culture of your church has meant a lot to a lot of people over lots of years. Even if they didn't articulate it as culture, it has the shared value of passionate history and shared story. So, assessing the culture should not be done lightly, but with respect and honor. It is a privilege and a humbling opportunity to assess a spiritual home.

Assessing does involve an honest, caring, objective look at the current reality. In the pages that follow you'll see helpful tools, but the tools are not designed to provide an authoritative, determinative score that will tell you exactly what to do; rather their purpose is to enable healthy discussion and discernment. In most cases, it is an assessment, not an obituary. The church remains a viable living spiritual organism as well as a fragile human organization.

There should be no finger-pointing, "I told you so," or one-upmanship. Avoid any perception that the culture assessment is somehow too punitive or something done to score points or further one's particular agenda regarding the church. Assessing a culture, therefore, should be done with a heart of gratitude and with eyes wide open to needed examination. Keep in mind, assessment is just one short journey through hallowed ground.

33

Good or bad characterizations are not particularly helpful. As we've mentioned, church cultures are made up of people and therefore there is always some element of good and bad. Focusing on that dichotomy can lead to judgmentalism. There is nothing wrong with affirming and celebrating your church's culture as good. But for our purposes it is better to assess the church in terms of whether it has a healthy culture and to accept with grace that there may be some areas that are not as healthy as people would like.

Unhealthy/Healthy

The concepts of healthy and unhealthy are not applied as a means of judgment, but as a qualitative determination as to whether the culture is supporting the mission and achieving its desired results. Is the current culture providing the expected and desired results? Unhealthy cultures tend to produce unintended perceptions that not only negatively affect performance but also enable an environment where there is little joy. In my (Yvette's) work as a business consultant, I occasionally encounter a company that has a stressful work environment but is also high performing. On the surface, that particular company looks like it has a healthy culture. But, if you look further, there are several unintended consequences that are caused by the stressful culture that are affecting profits and customer perception, such as high employee attrition, increased employee complaints to human resources, and high incidents of sick leave and short-term disability. At this point the cost of being high performing is too great and there is a need to address the unhealthy culture. A healthy culture promotes not only achieving goals but also oftentimes exceeding them.

In the church, a healthy culture may look like a church experiencing attendance growth, increased participation in Bible study, leadership teams fully engaged, and an appropriate level of volunteer support. It often results in frequent first-time guests because an on-fire congregation is recommending the church to friends and associates. There is a noticeable and compelling positive and enthusiastic atmosphere that naturally creates a welcoming environment that propels people into ministry and mission.

Effective culture assessments help get the congregation over the fear of pulling back the layers of the onion and ensure that the congregation sees the benefits of taking a good, honest look at its own heart while being committed to achieving long-term results in line with the vision and strategic goals of the church. Assessing your church's culture in terms of health creates a climate in which leadership can determine whether the culture needs to (a) improve in places where it may be weak or unhealthy, (b) change to become more healthy, and (c) better message the culture in the church and community if it is deemed to be healthy and appropriate for the church's life. Honor and search for ways the current reality of the church can be leveraged into a bridge to the future to meet the emerging needs of the community. Love the church but don't shy away from honest assessment. The culture may have been relevant and healthy and a great foundation for your church at one time, but has it lost its pizazz or is it no longer effective or even relevant for today?

Desired Results

Desired results form the basis for any cultural assessment. We can't just simply do an assessment as though we are evaluating performance. FIRST ask: "What are the desired results?" THEN assess the culture in light of actually getting the desired results. As Tom Smith and Roger Conners say in *Change the Culture, Change the Game*, "Your organization's culture determines your results."[2]

So, before you jump into a church culture assessment, be sure that leadership has grappled with the tough question, "What are our desired results?" One of those baked-in differences between connectional churches and independent churches is that the desired results are not the same. Not that one is better than the other; they are just different. And I'm not talking about theological or eschatological desired results. Most all Christian churches share the desired results of experiencing salvation, discipleship making, following Jesus, and changed lives. The desired results we are talking about have to do with church life.

Most connectional churches, like the UMC—while holding evangelism and reaching new people for Jesus as high values—also place a high priority on "other-than-church growth" values. Things like organization, structure, justice, inclusion, and laity involvement are simply approached in massively different ways than in more independent congregations as the "desired results" of church life. These desired results may change as the community changes, as the leadership of the church changes, or as circumstances of the community or the church change. That's why it's important to assess your culture frequently and without fear.

Assessment starts with desired results: One way to look at it is what percentage of your desired results (whatever they may be for your church) are you achieving? If you are achieving 75 to 100 percent, you probably don't need to change anything, including culture. If 50 to 75 percent, you should ask, "How can we better message our already strong culture?" If 25 to 50 percent, you should ask, "What can we tweak for improvement? How deep an assessment do we need to do to improve?" If under 25 percent, you'll want to determine what culture shifts are needed to get more on track. How thorough of a culture assessment will be beneficial? If much less than 25 percent, you probably need to do a major culture assessment/change process, and be alert to stagnation or possibly even a toxic culture brewing.

Intentional

Socrates said, "An unexamined life is not worth living," and we might add, "An unexamined culture is not worth building a ministry upon." We often find that church folk speak of their culture in flowery, general terms that they hope will be inspirational, but the truth is, what they speak about is aspirational. And, as is often said nowadays, "hope is not a strategy."

In countless cases, church members—for good reason—love their church. It has fed them, nourished them, inspired them, served them, become their social circle, and given them their identity. They know it's not perfect, but it is their church! Unfortunately, over time and myriad social changes, the way they see themselves in their Christian community is no longer the same way that others see them. To motivate a church to take a deep dive into who they really are, how they really operate, and what they really accomplish is a delicate process that requires intentionality.

There is no autocorrect button on church culture. Even when faced with measurable declines, changing demographics within and around the church, and a radically secularized and changing world, it is easy for members to assume the culture is fine. "We just need to get more young families in here" is a common refrain. Too often church leaders make the assumption that the culture of the church will "fix itself" in God's good timing. In some instances that may be true, but most of the time a church needs to be intentional about assessing and refreshing its culture. When assessing the church's culture is not done with intentionality, it will often simply appear to be disingenuous. And then members may often be skeptical and resistant because the randomness will come off as simply a way for "the pastor (or some other leader) to put their personal agenda on us." That is, it can be perceived by congregants as "targeted" at someone or a group that is doing something or not doing something the church should be doing. The church can easily begin to feel like they are victims of some new program aimed at changing them.

Notice that when a church does a capital campaign, no matter how they do it or what consultant they do it with, it is understood that it has to be done with intentionality and urgency. This means campaign planners develop measurable desired results; they publicize and work toward a timeframe; they create a leadership structure that begins with a few and spreads throughout the congregation with the intentionality of getting as many people involved as they can. The campaign itself sets the stage for a positive, successful atmosphere of "we can do this!" And it allows for the expectation that there may be future campaigns as growth and needs necessitate.

A church culture assessment is similar but harder. Let's face it, building a Family Life Center gets more attention than assessing our culture! But the process is the same: Leaders create a widely publicized framework to (a) identify desired results in light of the church's current reality; (b) establish a timeline answering who, when, how, and why questions; (c) assess the existing culture in positive ways through congregation-wide input; and (d) aim for results of the assessment that allow the church to see if and when the current culture needs to be shifted and/or reshaped.

In short, as we often say in our workshops, "It is easier to pull a rope than push a rope!" That is, intentionality means to create a vision and a way to pull the church into its future through a healthy culture . . . not push it into its future with pressure techniques and programs.

Ask

Ask honest questions frequently about how your church's culture is perceived by (a) church members, (b) potential prospects, (c) community leaders, and (d) people who have visited the church but chose not to affiliate.

Yvette led the Church for All People to begin assessing their culture by first asking deep questions. When the leadership of the Church of All People became intentional and had the courage to ask the difficult and candid questions, people were very direct and sincerely honest. One gentleman, without any intended malice, shared with leadership, "I am not ready for a black pastor." While very blunt and felt by many as harsh, this was the wake-up call the leadership team needed. It gave them insight into the culture of their church. What they believed was a loving culture ready to embrace people in the community was a loving culture but only to those from their past, not those in their future. There was a fear of the unknown. There was a culture of historical misperceptions. Very few had friends of a different ethnicity, and so the idea of coming together to worship seemed quite foreign to them. The question-asking revealed that the congregation was not—at least not yet—ready for a culture shift centered toward a diverse congregation. In asking the questions and listening closely to the answers, they could now better define the best path to evolve the culture of the church, correct some of the changes made in haste, and truly do a heart work before they could create a healthy multiethnic church culture, which they are now well on their way to achieving.

Another way to look at it isn't quantitatively (surveys, research, metrics) but qualitatively (observation, interviews, conversations): Are we noticing a drop in volunteerism or general happiness in the system? Are we feeling the effects of culture growing static? Is there something toxic going on? Asking good questions can help leaders get good, qualitative feedback, which is helpful in assessing the church culture.

Questions will help you focus on a clear picture of your church's culture. You may find the following "8 x 8 Exercise" a helpful guide for asking good church culture questions.

The 8 x 8 Exercise

Church culture often has a public face and sometime also a "below the surface" aspect that may be well hidden but detrimental. This exercise stimulates reflection and discussion. It is not a scientific tool, nor does it try to "score" your church's culture. It a way to talk about your church's public (and below-the-surface) culture, get a handle on it, and begin to figure out how to deal with it. Be honest and candid but not judgmental or condescending, please.

Step 1: (a) Write down 8 words you have heard people use when talking about an unhealthy culture. (b) Then write 8 words you have heard used when talking about a healthy culture.

Unhealthy:

Healthy:

Step 2: Now, which 4 words in each category come closest to describing your church's current culture . . .

when it is working well?

when it is working not so well?

Working Well:

Not So Well:

Step 3: Which words above characterize the public (and/or below-the-surface) culture right now?

Current Reality:

Step 4: Which words get closest to the kind of desired culture you would like to see?

Aspirational:

In the next chapter we share several good tools for assessing your church's culture. These tools have worked around the country, but they may not work for you, in your context, or at this time in your church's life. That's fine. We are not interested in getting you to buy in to everything we will share. Our hope, however, is that if you see a tool that you think wouldn't work for you and your church, it will at least spur your own creativity to come up with some other appropriate tool of your own creating.

When to Do a Culture Assessment

When is the right time to do a culture checkup? How healthy is your church right now? In the diagram on the following page, "Church Culture Check Up," you can see the most often cited reasons to do a culture checkup.

Knowing when to do a culture checkup can be guided by what's going on inside the heart and life of the church. In the diagram on the following page, "Common Symptoms of Church Cultures," you can take your pulse in a preliminary way to see what kind of assessment might be called for. What does a healthy church culture mean to you and your church? The following discussion exercise can stimulate honest conversation to get a clearer understanding about a healthy church culture.

CHURCH CULTURE *Check Up*

There are prescribed times in any organization—including a church—
when it would benefit from a culture checkup.

☐ **WHEN THERE IS A PASTORAL CHANGE**

Is the change involving a founder or long-tenured pastor leaving? A retirement? An abrupt
change due to ineffectiveness, mis-match, or behavioral issues? Or simply A more typical 3-7
year change?

☐ **WHEN DISRUPTING EXTERNAL INFLUENCES STRIKE**

Coronavirus, denominational uncertainty, social unrest, economic upheaval are examples of
pressures that create shock and turmoil.

☐ **WHEN DISTURBING INTERNAL ISSUES ERUPT**

A church endures culture changing pain when there is bad behavior or malfeance among
staff or laity.

☐ **WHEN GLACIER-LIKE CHANGES ERODE EFFECTIVENESS**

Sometimes a church isn't really aware of slow, generational declines or changes which
diminish relevancy and effectiveness, often resulting in the church no longer looking like its
community.

☐ **WHEN NEW & DIFFERENT RESULTS ARE DESIRED**

Leadership intentionally and strategically decides there needs to be a culture change to get
needed new and different results in its ministry and for its mission.

DIFFERENCE
MAKERS

COMMON SYMPTOMS
OF CHURCH *Cultures*

It is often said that the best way to take the temperature of a church is to put the thermometer in the leadership's mouth. While this is true and necessary, you can also take the temperature of a church's culture by observing the congregation's behavior. The following are common symptoms most often seen in the churches we work with. What is the cultural temperature of your church?

1.CULTURE IS UNHEALTY AND NEEDS TO BE CHANGED*
- Lack of joy; burdensome feel; sterile feel; maybe even toxic.
- Inwardly focused culture directs church resources, energy, and emphasis almost entirely on maintenance rather than its mission.
- A growing prevalence of complaining, criticizing, negativity and blaming while there is noticeable lack of personal responsibility and accountability.
- Downward trajectory of nearly all measurables in life of the church.

2.CULTURE IS OK BUT NEEDS TO BE STRENGTHENED
- Fatigue, but people dutifully "hanging in there."
- Stake holders feel proud of good things being done, but express lack of focus.
- A lethargic spirit of volunteerism; fewer and fewer people doing more and more work.
- Not many first- time guests and very few return.

3.CULTURE IS GOOD BUT NEEDS TO BE BETTER MESSAGED
- Leadership becomes aware of plateauing impact accompanied by desire to do better.
- Outwardly focused culture making a difference accompanied by desire to see exponential impact.
- Pleasant, "Feel-good" church family spirit accompanied by desire to become more welcoming and inviting to make a difference in the community.
- Church rightly focuses on its aspirational dreams; but frustrated over slow results.

*A complete cultural transplant may be needed and may work, but should only be considered in the most extreme of circumstances, such as in the strategic "Friendly takeover" of a struggling church by a larger, healthier church.

Earlier I mentioned reading the sports page and seeing how often a new coach begins the opening press conference with: "First, we've got to change the culture." Keep in mind the coach's venue is made up of paid (and most very highly paid) players, staff, and front office personnel. Similarly, the new CEO is dealing with paid employees.

In the church world, only a small percentage of the audience are paid staff; the overwhelming majority range from dedicated volunteers to backbench attenders to members in name only.

Let's acknowledge that changing a church's culture is categorically different from most other kinds of ventures. It requires a deep—and delicate—assessment done in understanding and understandable ways. And a pastor must never lose sight of the reality that many people have poured their time, treasure, and talents into the church over the years. When a pastor starts assessing the church's culture, it is common that the people in the church may interpret that as attacking the church, as ridiculing its customs, demeaning its practices, and diminishing its importance in *their* lives.

A "nice" church does not equal a healthy culture; a "friendly" church does not necessarily indicate a healthy culture; even a "loving" church does not mean a church's culture is healthy. Actually, at times those perceived attributes merely serve as masks hiding deeper, barely imperceptible culture problems. As the old saying goes about an inwardly focused church: "That church loved itself to death."

Even as specialists in church culture we cannot tell you what your church culture should be (although we will lift up some commonalities among healthy church cultures), and neither can anyone else.

A healthy church culture has several common features. One is that it enables an environment of growth. Several years ago when Bob Farr (now Bishop Bob Farr) popularized the Healthy Church Initiative, the opening session of the congregational workshop started with a simple statement: "Healthy things grow."

Please note that growth does not necessarily mean growth in average worship attendance, or membership, or budget. But it could be growth in spiritual maturity, or growth in discipleship, or growth in missional outreach, or growth in many other equally valuable variables. But it does mean that a healthy culture creates an environment of growth.

Healthy things grow, but let's be honest; not every growing thing is healthy. Think, tumor. Or the once fast-growing megachurch Mars Hill in Seattle that grew to enormous size but collapsed almost overnight because of an emerging toxic culture, which we highlighted in chapter 4.

Being a healthy church is absolutely critical for long-term viability. A church's health is what strengthens it to withstand times of crisis and sustains it in times of leadership change and even downward trends in church life. We've been talking about tools and techniques, but it is important not to overlook the power of the Holy Spirit.

In our experience, that is the God-sourced power that makes the culture last, long beyond any of us, for years to come. To endure doesn't mean the culture is static and never-changing! It does mean it is a God-breathed, living, vital organism that adapts when properly led and managed. While this is not intended as a theological book, and we acknowledge that people have differing views of and experiences with the Holy Spirit, a central tenant of United Methodism and Christianity worldwide is the primacy of the Holy Spirit to make a life-changing difference.

Chapter 6

Tools for Assessing
Your Church Culture

"The leader who understands and adapts to the organizational culture is
more likely to lead the church forward and enjoy the journey."
—Edgar H. Schein, *Organizational Culture and Leadership*

D
o you know a pastor who is gifted at "reading" culture? No doubt
they possess an excellent pastoral heart, preaching giftedness, and
leadership skills—but they also seem to have an innate ability to
read and respond well to the culture of their new church. Whether it stems
from EQ (emotional intelligence) or some other factor, that pastor almost
miraculously picks up on the clues emitting from the culture, which usually
leads to good things and a long tenure.

But as amazing as "reading the culture" is, it's different from a congregational assessment. Reading the culture is basically a solo enterprise; a congregational assessment is a corporate venture. An assessment is a deeper dive
related to the church's fruitfulness—or lack thereof—in getting the results
it desires to get. An assessment does more than just identify the culture; it
looks at the culture's origins, its expressions over time, how it got to be the
way it is, trends, ups and downs—all from a congregation-wide, neutral,
nonjudgmental perspective.

Sometimes that pastor who is gifted at reading the culture can actually
get in the way of congregational assessment. Why? Because when people
rely too much on a leader (especially a very persuasive leader) who trumpets
an above-average ability to read the culture, it can actually mask the pastor's

own blind spots. And it can unwittingly deprive the church from gaining new footholds in charting a new path into its future. Assessing your church's culture at various chapters in the church's life can be a blessing!

In the next few pages you'll see a number of excellent culture assessment tools, ranging from simple and easy-to-use to the more complete and complex. There is no one-size-fits-all approach. It takes introspection and common agreement among all parties. Discerning which of these tools may be most appropriate for your church usually includes an evaluation of how complex your congregation is and what kind of bandwidth in terms of energy and personnel you have at your disposal. These tools are designed to be simple and clear enough that a leader can use each tool to help teach and coach the church to understand and buy in to necessary targeted culture tweaks, perhaps more expansive shifts, or even major or total culture changes.

Churches do these kinds of surveys in different ways: some churches lean toward "all church" surveys, for instance; other churches aim the tools more toward leadership and/or designated teams. We have no recommendation as to which way to proceed, but our observation is that "all church" surveys seldom reveal any better insights than when the tools are used on a smaller group of leaders .

The Historical Classic Way of Assessing a Church Culture

Assessing church culture is not new, but the recent tsunami of change in the world and the church requires us to look at church culture change in new ways. Church leaders for generations have recognized that different sized churches require different leadership and exemplify different cultures. The following categories, commonly used by judicatory bodies, are from Arlin Rothauge, included in the Life and Leadership site:

1. The Primary Family Church (30–50 AWA [Average Worship Attendance]). The pastor's role is to manage the expectations and care for the family's needs, not to take charge.

2. The Extended Family Church (50–150 AWA). Like a clan or large close-knit family that has grown up and now has their own families. The pastor is treated as a new friend of certain members and invited to participate in activities.

3. The Family-Owned Enterprise Church (150–350 AWA). Like a family-owned business that has more structure and focus but is still very tied to the family. The pastor's role is more like that of a hired worker.

4. The Corporate Enterprise Church (350–800 AWA). Like a corporation. The pastor's role is more like that of a COO (chief operations officer), which is to give strong leadership to the organization while making certain the needs of members are met.

5. The Corporate Multi-enterprise Church (800–plus AWA) Like a franchised corporation that includes many different subgroups and ministries, each with its own focus and resources. The pastor's role is a CEO (chief executive officer) who sets the course and provides overall vision and leadership.

Many denomination supervisors have relied upon this kind of system to help match a potential pastor for a church of a specific size. And many young pastors rejoice at the chance to move from a "family-style" church to "corporate" church! These categorizations of churches based on size and the personality of congregations helped pastors better understand what to expect from serving any particular size church.

This model was widely used for decades and still has important value. But as churches deal with an unprecedented pace of societal, denominational, and generational changes, the movement from pre-1980s *characterizing* culture to post-1990s *changing* the culture has risen in importance.

And one last note before we get into our culture assessment and change tools. It is inescapable that demographics will affect any church's culture, and changing demographics may reveal the need for culture change. Are the demographics in the community around your church showing the population as declining? Growing? Aging? Changing? Excellent demographic companies (such as Mission Insight) and their various trend reports must be included as a foundational level of any culture assessment.

When it comes to tools to assess your church's culture, the simplest and easiest one (see below) is simply what we call "'The Feel' of Our Church's Culture," which takes into account not only the prevalent attitude and spirit but also the physical aspects such as the condition of the facilities, location and landscaping, parking capacity, and traffic patterns.

"The Feel" of our Church's Culture
"Feel" .... Even if someone can't describe it, they 'sense it'.

What is "feel" of the space?

Focused - Not so much

How well does it tell the story of the church's ministry? What kind of story does it tell?
- Architecture? Kept up? Landscaping?
- What kind of hallway and office decor?
- Do hallways and space message the ministry and passion of the congregation?
- Is parking sufficient?

What is the "feel" of the place?

Friendly - Not so much

How do people treat one another? How do they meet new people? Laughter? Fun? Joy? Does it seem 'permission giving' to initiatives and new ministries?

What is the "feel" of the pace? Is there 'buzz' & excitement?

Energetic- Not so much

What would you add to get a sense of the "feel" of your church?

_____ _____

++++++++++++++++++++++++++++

Other ways to "assess" your church's culture:

1. Online tools (ie. Readiness 360)
2. Ask & Listen
3. Pay Attention
4. Other ways that you utilize?

Note: It is seldom just "one culture" ... Almost every organizational culture has a network of sub-cultures operating at the same time.

While this tool is the simplest and can be used in a variety of ways to secure feedback, in many ways its importance cannot be overestimated. Many people make their church-going decision based on "the feel" of the place when they first arrive!

A slightly deeper tool is "The 'Firm Foundation' Assessment of Church Culture" (see the next page). We have watched spellbound as congregants sitting around tables dive into deep conversation about these items and share in profound ways!

We have shared simple principles and tools for assessing your church's culture. This can be done by virtually any church, but perhaps you are in a setting where you feel like an outside organization can further your objectives.

Our approach to creating and/or changing culture is what we detail in the remaining pages of this book. So, now you have assessed the current culture; it is time to look at how to create the culture you want. The remainder of this book is to teach you the "See It, Say It, Show It, Grow It" model of creating culture.

But wait! What if you happen to be at one of those churches that has not been able to keep up with its community, that has not been able to penetrate its mission field, that sees most of its dwindling membership grow older and more fatigued, that has an aging building and fewer resources? You've seen those churches that have declined for years, but the remaining members are emotionally connected to their church in a way that thwarts objective decision-making. What if assessing the culture leads to the discernment that the only way to be God-honoring in determining the future requires a wholesale culture change, like closing and re-opening in a merged situation with new identity and direction?

Every year in America, thousands of churches close. It is always sad and almost always emotional. Members frequently ask: "What did we do wrong?" Or, "Why are they wanting to shut us down?" Or they say, "Over my dead body will the conference close my church!"

The *"Firm Foundation"*
Assessment of Church Culture

"How firm a foundation!" proclaims the ancient hymn to encourage us even when facing "deep waters, fiery trials, or being overwhelmed and abandoned."

Here's an important question: Is the foundation of my church able to withstand being shaken by Covid-19? Denominational uncertainties? Responding to cries for social justice? Our foundation is in the Lord; a great culture reveals that foundation and enables the church to get stronger even when its foundations are shaken! It points to "Things unshakeable!" Hebrews 12

Look at daily life inside the church; then apply the "Firm Foundation" approach ... it can be a helpful way to look at your church's culture and impact!

F3 – Definite strength
F2 – OK but could be better
F1 – Needs Improvement

Simply place a # value next to each F: (Encourage other leaders do the same for healthy discussion.)

_____ **F — FUTURE** *(Hallway talk more about future than the past)*

_____ **F — FOCUS** *(Clear sense of focus as to God's calling on the church)*

_____ **F — FAITH** *(Hallway conversations sprinkled with spirituality and faith stories)*

_____ **F — FIRE** *(Noticeable passion about what church is doing and what God is up to)*

_____ **F — FREEDOM** *(Unleashed passion! Entrepreneurial! New things in new ways!)*

_____ **F — FRUITFULNESS** *(Celebrating life-change & difference-making accomplishments)*

_____ **F — FRESH** *(Fresh ideas, fresh faces, fresh spirit abound)*

_____ **F — FUN** *(Staff, leadership, and laity have fun being the church)*

_____ **F — FAMILY** *(Appropriate sense of intimacy, connection, and mutual support)*

_____ **F — FINANCES** *(Strong sense of generosity, stewardship, financial trust)*

_____ **F — FUNDAMENTALS** *(Biblical guidance, healthy structure, relevant application.)*

In my ministry career, I (Jim) have worked with many "churches at the crossroads" of dying or of making major if not total changes to keep the church relevant to the changing demographic of the community. Although I am not a church sociologist and can't fully explain the dynamics that lead a church to cease to exist, I do believe that a healthy culture cannot grow in an unhealthy body. Even when we remind churches on the brink of closing that not one of the famous churches the apostle Paul founded, preached to, or wrote about is still alive today, congregation members are flooded with grief and often anger.

Before making hasty decisions about struggling churches, most conferences employ the biblical principle found in Luke 13:6-9 (NIV):

> Then he told this parable: "A man had a fig tree growing in his vineyard, and he went to look for fruit on it but did not find any. So he said to the man who took care of the vineyard, "For three years now I've been coming to look for fruit on this fig tree and haven't found any. Cut it down! Why should it use up the soil?"" "Sir,' the man replied, 'leave it alone for one more year, and I'll dig around it and fertilize it. If it bears fruit next year, fine! If not, then cut it down.'"

That is to say, conference and church leadership will do almost anything to keep from having to close a church. But unfortunately, it occasionally happens. That's when I pray for a healthy denominational culture, shared by all member churches alike, that demonstrates the end is never the end! We are Easter people! God can and will take our current reality and bring from it transformational healing.

Part Two

Church Culture: How to Change It and Create It

Chapter 7

"See It, Say It, Show It, Grow It" Overview

The most compelling reason to work on your culture? Culture produces results.
—Roger Connors, *Change the Culture, Change the Game*

Culture change, like any idea with the word *change* in it, is a phrase that often brings about anxiety and even dread, even in circumstances when it is clearly needed. So pastors, be sure you recognize that those whom you lead can be nervous and express negative, even contrarian behaviors about even the thought of culture change. It's not personal; it's natural! So as directly as you can, "turn unknowns into knowns," in Tony Jeary's words.[1] Be reassuring about all aspects of the culture change process. Cast a doable, positive vision and then one by one respond to (without reacting to) every expressed fear or concern.

As a result of assessing your culture, courses of action are explored: Is our culture healthy and strong, but we just need to message it better? Is our culture stuck or static, but we just don't know how—or don't have the will to—change it? Is our culture becoming a negative for us, and that's the reason we are declining? Is our culture toxic, filled with conflict and negativity that derails anything positive we try to accomplish? Your answers will shape the way you make changes to your culture.

A quick note here: Readers perhaps know that our company, Church Difference Makers, does nationwide work on pastoral transitions (see our book, *The Changeover Zone: Successful Pastoral Transitions*.[2] In Changeover Zone workshops we are often asked about how the new pastor coming into a church should deal with the church's culture. Friends, it took a whole book to get deep into all those principles, but suffice it to say that when a new pastor arrives, there will always be some culture shifts!

This is not a new observation. In the 1980s, influential church consultant Lyle Schaller observed that when a new pastor comes, a church should expect a new vision. Schaller said, "Once a new vision emerges there must be new structures to support that new vision, and one must make sure that traditions, values, customs and habits (culture) are consistent with the new vision."[3]

As a new pastor you are not called to demean your predecessor's ministry or the church's existing culture. But as your ministry unfolds, you will surface your own sense of vision and mission. Following principles in this book, proceed respectfully, carefully, and strategically.

God, in creating the world, also created the first culture. Culture creation can be traced throughout history. I (Yvette) do this ministry because I have seen and known the power of culture in every institution and across the ages.

The Lord prescribed a culture of obedience and reverence to him that would provide for humankind to live in harmony with all of creation. God, with great intentionality and care, created every living thing and gave humankind dominion over it all.

This culture—our paradise of heaven on earth—however, would not live on forever. Humankind's freewill and ability to make choices led to a change. Eve was presented with a choice to do life differently, and there was an immediate culture shift. The way of life for Adam and Eve and humanity was forever changed. Life went from the Garden of Eden where everything was provided for humankind by God to the hardships of having to work the land and provide for ourselves while still in relationship with God. The "how"—how humankind would live out their days—was forever changed. It was a massive culture shift.

As we read the stories of the Bible, there is great emphasis on describing the culture of the day, because the culture had such an influence on every aspect of the people's lives and their relationship with God. We see in these stories culture shifts large and small.

In the New Testament, much is made of the culture during the time of Jesus's ministry and the relationship of the Jews and Gentiles. The laws, as interpreted by the Pharisees and Sadducees significantly influenced the prevailing culture of their communities. Jesus's coming was to disrupt the prevailing culture and establish a new covenant—a new culture. It is from this shift that the "church" was born.

Culture is always creating, re-creating and changing to meet the needs of a specific time and specific circumstances. That is not a bad thing, nor does it run counter to our understanding of "the unchanging God" or whatever absolutes we attribute to the Kingdom of God. Culture change is not an attack on God. Nor should it be seen in the local church as an affront to that church's history or its desire to honor and obey God. Culture is the vehicle to carry the church's highest values in its quest to do the work of God and make new disciples for Jesus. Culture—and its creation and re-creation—is powerful, historical, and biblical.

This chapter begins to lay out the sequential steps to culture change, so let's talk practically about how leaders create the culture they want to get the results the church needs.

The most fruitful way to create the church culture you want is to implement the "See It, Say It, Show It, Grow It" process (see the Step Up Culture Change Model on the following page) and be open to learning a culture creation process that can make a difference in your church. As we lean into this process, we will first share a brief summary and then in the following chapters detail it thoroughly.

The "See It" phase of the Step Up Culture Change Model is a dual track of (a) seeing your current culture in assessments through tools we described in the previous chapter, which includes agreeing on the desired results leaders want to see; and (b) seeing your own culture words that you will message constantly as you create culture.

The "Say It" phase uses your culture words to knit together a unified team of staff and key leaders who are on a common mission to message the culture constantly to achieve the desired results the church has identified.

The "Show It" phase spreads the culture throughout leadership and volunteers by adopting behaviors and practices that are to be front and center in all aspects of the church's life.

The "Grow It" phase is to embed the culture via consistent messaging throughout the entire congregation and the community so that your agreed-upon culture reveals and establishes the identity of the church.

This model helps a church to grow because it messages to everyone a culture that is clear, healthy, and compelling! The "See It, Say It, Show It, Grow It" process helps you systematically and strategically gain clarity on the "why" and "how" and "when" to implement needed culture change.

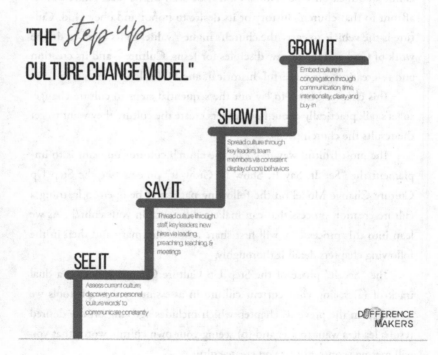

"THE *step up* CULTURE CHANGE MODEL"

SEE IT
Assess current culture; discover your personal 'culture words' to communicate constantly

SAY IT
Thread culture through staff, key leaders, new hires via leading, preaching, teaching, & meetings

SHOW IT
Spread culture through key leaders, team members via consistent display of core behaviors

GROW IT
Embed culture in congregation through communication time, intentionality, clarity and buy-in

DIFFERENCE MAKERS

How Jesus Modeled It

The genesis of our "See It, Say It, Show It, Grow It" process of culture change was Jesus himself. Jesus modeled this process throughout Scripture.

The "See It" phase happened early in Jesus's life when he went into the wilderness for forty days, and later in his ministry when he slipped away alone in the garden of Gethsemane. I imagine that whatever else happened in those times, Jesus looked deep into his soul. He no doubt delved into his calling and his relationship to his heavenly father. My guess is that he found this time to ask deep questions of himself and to wrap himself in prayer, meditation, and spiritual surrender. Likewise, getting away and being alone for a period of time to find your personal culture words is not only a blessing; it is also a necessity. In those times you begin to discover those words or short phrases that emerge from your heart and clarify your deepest values, desires, and commitment; those words that echo from God's call on your life; those words that frame your very understanding of ministry.

Of course, throughout the New Testament narrative, we see that Jesus saw the current religious culture and displayed his mastery of assessing through his teachings and observations like, "render unto Caesar what is Caesar's and to God what is God's." His assessment hit the frustration level when he rode into Jerusalem and turned over the tables in the temple. There are countless other teachings when Jesus is seen assessing the current culture. The result is summarized in Acts when his disciples are said to be "turning the world upside down!"

The "Say It" phase can be seen in his teachings, parables, miracles, and recorded conversations with his disciples and others throughout the Gospels. He used parables to connect people to the word of God and to make it relevant and relatable. The "Say It" part is about helping people embrace words for full understanding. The parables of the prodigal son, the good Samaritan, the mustard seed, the coin, and the lost sheep and new wine were all ways that Jesus found creative and effective ways to state points to achieve understanding and give people greater insight into the word and ways of God. He was using storytelling to reveal critical points to people to influence change in their culture.

The "Show It" phase can be capsulized in the Sermon on the Mount in which his words began to paint a picture of the Beatitudes that would mark his beloved community. The "Show It" phase was highlighted when he set the example of servanthood by washing the feet of his disciples and by demonstrating once and for all the sacrificial nature of commitment when he showed to all that he was "all in" and went to the cross.

The "Grow It" phase had already begun when it was evident that he had a large and dedicated following. But it was concretized not only with his resurrection but also with his intentionality in sending the Holy Spirit to guide and motivate his followers to continue to grow the Pentecostal experience. The book of Acts is rich with all the ways the "Grow It" phase of culture happened because of the ministry of Jesus Christ.

The goal of the "See It, Say It, Show It, Grow It" model is to enable a church to create or change its culture. Why? Because all too often churches default to changing things in the hopes of changing its culture to achieve desired results. The Church for All People defaulted to the "big thing" approach in part because the senior pastor and leadership couldn't see the culture they actually wished to instill that would get their desired results. Here is how Yvette reflects upon this episode in their story:

The Church for All People moved quickly, without a proper assessment of the existing culture, to put "things" in place to attract those within the community. Therefore, decisions were made and changes put in place that created tension and uneasy feelings within the staff and some of the very tenured members. Remember, in the church world, culture is attached to the heart and passions of people, as well as to the behaviors and practices of the people.

As how ministry was done began to change, feelings were hurt and people felt isolated and not engaged. Many felt they were losing "their" church. What a full assessment of the culture revealed was that people had perceptions of what changes in the ethnic makeup in the church would mean, and they were fearful. Many of those perceptions were false and needed to be dealt with lovingly and honestly to truly move the church forward in a healthy manner. It would mean a year of working with the hearts of people, changing the false narratives, and ending the cross-racial appointment to allow time for the culture to change. Because the culture was not ready for such a shift, it was creating an unhealthy environment for both the pastor and the congregation. Spoiler alert: After the assessment and a few years of working with the heart of people, the church ultimately did make the culture shift and is now welcoming to all in the community and beginning to grow again within a healthy culture.

Once the senior pastor and leadership could begin to "see it," then they could create the culture needed by employing the "See It, Say It, Show It, Grow It" culture change model. It is worth a little time to connect the dots of a church's culture and its vision.

Culture and Vision

The overview is simply to connect the dots of the relationship of vision with culture. What is your vision of God's call upon your life? Your church? What desired results do you envision for your church? (More first-time guests? More returning guests? More confessions of faith? More generousity? etc.) What is the current reality that you see when honestly assessing your church? What missional needs do you see that expand your vision when you look at your church and community context?

A pastor we worked with shared this telling conversation:

Pastor: "I needed a vision, but all I got was a view."

Me: "Not sure I understand. You mean you had a point of view?"

Pastor: "No; it was more like I was on a balcony watching my church and my ministry parading down a street; I had no control. I just watched, sometimes with amazement, sometimes with disgust. Thank you. You helped me see I was watching the parade and wondering what things to change. Now I know what I have control over; what I can change is the culture. Then things will take care of themselves."

Culture not only springs from vision but also is what turns vision into reality. It is true that church culture is not your vision, purpose, or mission statement. But while it is not any one of these important foundational elements of a church, it requires a blending of all of them.

We have summarized how this blending happens, so in the following chapters we will detail the process more precisely.

Chapter 8

See It: Finding Your Culture Words

Culture in your church is the unwritten rules of behavior.
—Stephen Blandino, *Creating Your Church's Culture*

Throughout this book we have been sharing definitions and characteristics of the church's culture. For example, Aubry Malphurs defines a church's congregational culture as "the unique expression of the interaction of the church's shared beliefs and its values which explain its behavior in general and displays its unique identity in particular."[1]

True, your church's culture is our topic. However, the path to getting a clear understanding of the church's culture runs through your own heart and soul as the leader. There is no shortcut; getting clear about your church's culture goes hand in hand with getting clear about your personal culture. The following process demonstrates an effective way.

Your Personal Culture Words

In the previous chapter we talked about one track of "seeing it": assessing the church's culture. The other track is the lead pastor discovering her or his own culture words and then messaging them throughout the congregation. Let's turn now to this track: how to discover and then message your personal culture words.

A lead pastor's culture words are a set of a few words (two or three usually) or short phrases that identify what the pastor values highly and form the basis of their own expression of culture. These are words that a leader sprinkles into conversation and intentionally messages to others regularly and repeatedly in a way that, over time, becomes natural, expected, and effortless. This seems so simple and so obvious that you'd think every pastor would be able to do this. But here's what happens: A pastor gets so deep into the weeds of ministry, and so weary from balancing all the demands of a leader, and so slowly numbed to the pressure-cooker frustrations of the changing world and changing church today, that the pastor can unfortunately and almost invariably forget even why he or she is in ministry.

The first step in discovering your culture words is to set aside time alone—like Jesus modeled—to intentionally work on this exercise of finding (or rediscovering) your personal culture words. Set aside dedicated time to get away for the sole purpose of reflecting. An overnight retreat is best, at least a few hours to be alone to invite God's spirit to work inside of you. If nothing else, this exercise will strengthen you as a leader during this time of extreme challenges within the world and church. As the missionary E. Stanley Jones used to say, "If we have not that which is above us, within us, we soon fall to that which is around us."

Getting alone time seems harder to accomplish than ever, and probably more important that ever. *Church Leaders* magazine reported on a recent Westpath survey with this glaring headline: "United Methodist Pastors Feel Worse and Worry More Than a Decade Ago." Beginning the article with these uncomforting words: "UMC clergy have been through the wringer in recent years, with a worldwide pandemic, a church schism and the ongoing decline of one of the nation's largest Protestant denominations." The Wespath survey of 1,200 UMC clergy found that "half have trouble sleeping, a third feel depressed and isolated, half are obese, and three quarters are worried about money."[2]

If for no other reason than your mental/physical/emotional/spiritual well-being, this exercise is used as a further reason to get some time away. This exercise should not be rushed. As you meditate, as you pray, as you turn to Scripture, as you read good books, think of and explore three or four words (or short phrases) that truly describe who you are. These words come from your deepest inner self; they reflect your personality and reveal your soul. These words are not intended to impress anyone or be your aspirational wish list of what you would like to be. Just be authentic in who you are.

When a leader can clearly articulate and consistently message her or his culture words, it allows the congregation to rally around and buy in to common purpose and direction. Your culture words are the hinge upon which the doors open to effective ministry. It is what frames and forms a church's current ministry identity, core values, and unifying way of how it goes about doing what it does. They are, as you will see later in this short course on church culture, what threads and embeds the desired culture throughout the congregation and community. See the tool on the following page, Finding My Culture Words, to help guide you in finding your personal culture words.

The second step is found in this most critical reflection question (and perhaps the most important question): "What biblical story helps me make sense of my life story?" It is critical that your culture words spring from Scripture. Why? Because if they don't, your culture words will be perceived in the congregation as nothing more than your personal agenda you are trying to overlay onto the church.

So while you are reflecting in your alone time, remember that the starting point to finding your culture words that help create culture is God's Word. What is a favorite, foundational, biblical story that, if you dig deep into your own soul and your own personal understanding of ministry, becomes your story? What story stirs your soul and reminds you of why you answered a call to ministry in the first place? Chances are that the story forms and informs the culture you will want to create in your church.

Every pastor's story is unique. I do not know what yours is, or may become, but here is mine, and why it is so important to me as I create culture in the church and teach others to do so. In the early years of my pastorate in the church I led for eighteen years, it was a tough go. Circumstances arose that nearly derailed that young church start as I was becoming its second pastor following a beloved founder. I often heard people say, "I don't know if we are going to make it. We'll need a miracle." In our work over the last ten years as consultants with troubled churches, we often hear that phrase, "To survive, our church needs a miracle!"

Finding My Culture Words

Set aside a few hours to be alone to reflect. This exercise should not be rushed. Think of three or four words (or short phrases) that truly describe who you are. These words come from your deepest inner self; they reflect your personality and reveal your soul. These words are not intended to impress anyone or be your aspirational wish list of what you would like to be. Just authentic in who you are.

*When a leader can clearly articulate and consistently message her/his 'Culture Words' it allows the congregation to rally around and buy-in to common purpose and direction. Your culture words are the **first step** in what frames and forms a church's current ministry identity, core values, and unifying way of how it goes about doing what it does. They are what threads and embeds the desired culture throughout the congregation and community.*

Here are a few self-reflection questions that may help find your culture words:

- What did (does) God see in me to call me into ministry?

- What lights my fire?

- What keeps me going?

- What propels me forward?

- What about me inspires others?

- What biblical story helps me make sense of my life story?

- When thinking about my approach to ministry: "I like to have _____; I need to have _____; People often describe my personality as _____.

- When thinking about my life & ministry, core values that emerge are:

A first list of my culture words (may be revised as we go along):

1.

2.

3.

In 2009, I personally did the exercise we are sharing with you now, and the biblical story I settled on is a story of how to have a miracle in a church. It's the story of Elisha who was the great successor to the major prophet Elijah. Elisha is well known for being a central character in what many of the Old Testament refer to as the so-called minor miracle stories.

That is, they're really cool miracles, but you wonder why they are there anyway. But they are there, and they are worth us remembering. This particular story is about Elisha (whose name in Hebrew means "our salvation") and is found in 2 Kings 6:1-7. Let me show you how it provides an excellent guide on how to have a miracle in the life of a church.

> The company of the prophets said to Elisha, "Look, the place where we meet with you is too small for us. Let us go to the Jordan, where each of us can get a pole; and let us build a place there for us to live."
> And he said, "Go."
> Then one of them said, "Won't you please come with your servants?"
> "I will," Elisha replied. And he went with them.
> They went to the Jordan and began to cut down trees. As one of them was cutting down a tree, the iron axhead fell into the water. "Oh, my lord!" he cried out. "It was borrowed!"
> The man of God asked, "Where did it fall?" When he showed him the place, Elisha cut a stick and threw it there, and made the iron float. "Lift it out," he said. Then the man reached out his hand and took it. (NIV)

Admittedly, I am not a biblical scholar, but I am confident my interpretation would pass the examination of a scholarly exegesis. And you will see that it provides an excellent guide on how to have a miracle in the life of a church.

This story is an example of a biblical story becoming your story for the purpose of creating culture, and this is the way I used it for almost eighteen years to create culture in my congregation:

- I preached this story as a sermon at my church repeatedly and regularly.

- I taught it time and time again whenever I had the chance at meetings.

- I utilized it as a part of vetting potential new staff hires.

- I championed it whenever we had a new class of lay servant leaders beginning their time in office.

The reason I exegete this story so often is to reinforce the church's culture regularly, because—remember this truth—culture leaks. You have to constantly work on refilling it.

So here is my biblical story. Yours no doubt will be different and unique to you. But whatever biblical story forms the core of your ministry, teach it, preach it, and share it regularly. Your good friends in the church and longtime attenders may even laugh at you. "Oh, here comes the Elisha story again," is a comment I sometimes heard made in good will. But a first-time guest or even a rather new member may not have heard it before. So I take the risk and make this sermon at least an annual occurrence.

Verse 1: *The company of the prophets said to Elisha,*

Here's the setting: "The company of the prophets." I'm not a Bible scholar, but I think I have this right. Prophets used to have a following that would go with them, and it was like their congregation. So "the company of the prophets" means their church folk.

"Look, the place where we meet with you is too small for us."

The company of the prophets said to Elisha, "Look, the place where we meet with you is too small for us." Now that's the first thing I always stressed to my church, especially among staff and lay leadership. Ministry is always about growth. It may be about numerical growth. It may be about spiritual growth. It may be about the growth and maturity of a person's service. It may be about growth in a person's capacity to love others. It's always about growth.

So the setting of this minor miracle story in the Old Testament is that the prophet's folk present him with a problem: "Look, this place is just too small for us."

Verse 2: *"Let us go to the Jordan, where each of us can get a pole; and let us build a place there for us to meet."*

Note that the story begins to unfold in a way that speaks to organizational behavior and culture. I tell the staff at my church and our leadership:

"Its okay for you to come to me with a problem, but only if you have a solution in mind.

The solution that we ultimately may pick may not be the one you suggest. But here's a key component of culture. You see, if people feel free just to come with problems (such as the roof is leaking or our children's ministry coordinator is really messed up), people begin to think negatively. However, when you are intentional about insisting and acculturating people to always bring a solution, you begin to change from negative thinking to more positive thinking. It creates a whole different environment in which to work and participate in church life.

A little backstory: I went into the ministry when I was in high school under the great old missionary, E. Stanley Jones. He was in his early eighties when I went to work for him, so he could say this and get away with it: "You know my wife doesn't mind if occasionally I glance at an attractive young lady as long as I continue to gaze at her." "The problem," Brother Stanley said, "is when I get my glances and my gazes turned around!"

That is a cultural truth of the church. As church professionals and leaders, we are always dealing with problems, because problems abound. But, we are called to just glance at the problems of our ministry and to gaze at the promise and possibilities in Jesus Christ. What happens is, as clergy and key leaders, we can begin to get our glances and our gazes turned around. We begin only to glance at the promise and possibilities and to gaze at all the problems. When gazing at problems consumes leaders, morale spirals downward and soon wonderful church leaders become fatigued. Some even begin to look for a way out of leadership instead of looking for ways through problems.

What do key leaders and pastors do? They solve problems. Your members go to meeting after meeting during which you discuss problem after problem. If we're not conscious about it, we begin to focus on the problems and rarely lift up the promise of Jesus Christ to our people.

It is so important to get our glances and our gazes in the right order. Hear me clearly. I'm not suggesting pretending we don't have problems, nor am I suggesting we not deal with the problems head on. I suggest that we keep the glances and gazes in a productive order. To summarize this principle: One way to begin to shift the culture of your church to become more positive is to invoke the principle of, "If you bring a problem, bring a solution as well." The solution you bring may not be the one decided upon, but it gets staff members and church members thinking about solution more than the problem.'

And he said, "Go."

When they came up with their solution (go to the river and cut some poles for a larger space), Elisha answered them with one of the Bible's great words: "Go!" May I be so bold as to suggest that pastors go to serve and lead churches and they are supposed to get things done. They are leaders. And now, that doesn't mean they are kings or princesses or dictators, but we need pastors who have the courage and the wisdom and the ability to say, "Go." We've got to jump-start some things and do some things, but do the right things. That's why so many well-intentioned pastors focus on "things" that need to be done and end up wearing themselves out. Remember that "church culture is not the sum total of the things we do; it is the launchpad for everything we do." True, leaders must move the church forward, but it starts with creating a great culture that then leads to doing the right things.

Verse 3: *Then one of them said, "Won't you please come with your servants?"*

I hope the importance of this question does not escape you. It's the question that congregation members are asking pastors all the time in all sorts of ways, verbally and nonverbally, overtly and subtly. While congregants are looking for leadership, their interest isn't that you are good at identifying a direction and building momentum to say, "Go." The question is, "Are you with us?" Our people are not likely to go where we will not go. A clear culture messages partnership and shared responsibility, done with joy and excitement.

I well remember having to reshape and refocus my own ministry at a time when our church made the decision to become a church for the unchurched. That meant I would need to prioritize my time in a way that would not allow me be as active as I may have wanted to be within the structures and realm of our annual conference, because if my passion was to reach unchurched people, I decided that I must spend my time with unchurched people. And that's what I did because that's who I was called to serve. Our church wouldn't become a church to reach the unchurched unless they saw I was passionate about loving and living among the un-churched. I had to "go with them" and rearrange my priorities to make it happen if we were to maintain a culture of integrity.

Verse 4: *"I will,"* Elisha replied. And he went with them.
A culture in which ministry is clearly seen as partnership, as teamwork, as mutual dedication was created that day by Elisha and can be created by each and every one of us regularly.
They went to the Jordan and began to cut down trees.
Verse 5: *As one of them was cutting down a tree, the iron axhead fell into the water. "Oh no, my lord!" he cried out. "It was borrowed!"*

So hear how this story continues: They went down to the Jordan and began to cut down trees; and as one of them was cutting down a tree, the iron ax head slipped off the handle and splashed into the water. Biblical scholars do observe that this is one of the few times the word *iron* is actually used in the scripture. So obviously the writer wanted us to know this was iron. This was metal. This was something heavy. As one of them was cutting down the tree, the iron ax head fell into the water. "Oh no, my lord!" he cried out, "It was borrowed!"

This is a fun scene to picture. They're chopping down poles, and dur-ing one guy's backswing his iron ax head falls off and into the river. And he cries out, "Oh, my God, it's borrowed." Now here is why he is crying out. He had borrowed it from a friend or acquaintance, and because of that and the responsibility it implied, it meant a great deal to him. He valued it. For whatever reason, it caused him to cry out in agony. This is the first clue to discover your own personal "culture words." What is it in your ministry that you personally value so much that, *if it was gone*, you would cry out, "Oh, my God, it's gone!" You see, what you value above all else is what you would cry out to God about, "It's gone." What you value most personally in your ministry deserves to be known in the congregation, and that is what will become the springboard for clarifying and creating the culture of the church during your season of leadership.

Confirming Your Culture Words

Cultural communication is about asking questions. . . .
—William Vanderbloemen, *Culture Wins*[3]

My culture words are (a) *creative*, (b) *passionate*, and (c) *relevant*. Anyone who knows me or sees me work can see how important these words are to me. There is no doubt that if I somehow settled into doing ministry that wasn't creative, that lacked absolute passion, that seemed so irrelevant that I was just leading a church going through the motions, I would cry out to God in agony!

What you value most in ministry is your iron ax head. When you can identify that, you are well on your way to knowing the culture that God is calling you to set in the life of your church. Because what you value most—what is gut-level important in ministry—is what God put in you as part of your spiritual gift mix and calling.

I have a cherished friend in ministry who answered his call to God during the turbulent civil rights movement in Alabama. Social justice and a ministry of compassion fueled his passion to serve and to say yes to ministry. But one day he recounted to me in tears that it had been so long since he had acted on those impulses that he had forgotten who he was and why he was in ministry. Is it any wonder that his professional life had drifted from one church to another, lacking true passion and seeing little effectiveness? Once he got in touch again with his "iron ax head," he went on to great creativity and effectiveness in ministry, forging a forward-thinking church.

Remember, only you can determine what your iron ax head is, what the words are that will communicate it when you cast vision to accomplish it. Only you can know what it is that most deeply motivates you, moves you, shapes you.

God saw something in you—your unique personality, your passion, your quirks, your skill set, your relational capacity, your caring smile—*something* that God needed and still needs in this world today.

So let me encourage you to think about taking some deep time of soul-searching, prayer, and appropriate spiritual disciplines to get back in touch with what God originally saw in you and why God called you into ministry. Don't be embarrassed; it happens to almost everyone: we get so deep in the weeds of doing ministry, of building a career, of being effective . . . , that we lose track of our ax head.

Then (using the tool "Finding My Culture Words") identify three or four words or short phrases that speak to you in a way that reminds you again of what it is you value most.

As I mentioned earlier, for me, those three words are the words around which I have framed my whole ministry: *creative, passionate, relevant*. Those iron ax head words—when fully authentic, when messaged well, when accepted by and embedded within the church—can be the culture of your church for the season in which you are the pastor. Just remember: Teach that culture everywhere and all the time. In the remainder of this book you will learn effective ways to do just that.

Your iron ax head words probably won't be the same as mine; they may be the same as those of your best friends, or the pastor of the church down the street. This is not the time to try to be unique and different. Your iron ax head words are simply words that describe you and what you value most in ministry, Why you answered a call to the ministry, and what you would cry out to God about if they were not present and prominent in your ministry.

Your iron ax head words are your words, and they are what you value the most. What is it, if it were gone, you would cry out, "Oh, my God! Oh, my God!" Personally, I feel like I would refuse to pastor a church that would not be creative. I just don't want to pastor a church that's not passionate about its ministry. If I pastor a church, and we lose our cultural relevance, I would cry out, "Oh, my God. What am I wasting my time for?"

You see, those are my words. I don't know what yours would be: maybe family, maybe enthusiasm, maybe excitement, maybe fun, maybe mission. Only you will know. But find it and message it strategically.

If you don't know what your iron ax head is, you don't have any chance of teaching what you value most to your congregation. And all too often our people don't know what we value as pastors so much that we would cry out to God, "Oh, it's gone!" If they don't know your passion, they are not likely to catch it, and it is unlikely to form the basis of your church's culture.

Remember! Your personal culture words are not intended to be thrust upon a congregation in a dictatorial way; they are, however, to be presented in compelling ways to the church, with an openness to being modified for the context and needs of the congregation.

But back to Elisha's story!

Verse 6: *The man of God asked, "Where did it fall?"*

Then Elisha asked, "Where did it fall?" The Bible teaches early on that the best of leadership is not solely to come up with answers but to ask the right questions. Before you begin to articulate the culture you want to see in the life of your church, you have to ask a lot of questions of your church and your community. "Where did it fall?" sets the tone for asking important questions as part of your culture.

When he showed him the place, Elisha cut a stick and threw it there, and made the iron float.

What a miracle! An iron ax head floated! Here is how it happened: Elisha cut a stick and threw it into the water and the iron ax head floated to the top. For me, this is one of the passages that is as instructive for what it doesn't say as much as for what it does say. Perhaps I am taking some liberties with Scripture here, but notice it doesn't say that

- Elisha and some other guy found a huge stump and hoisted it up on their shoulders and struggled back to the river and threw it down hoping that it would hit the water with such force it that it would create some kind of plunging action and maybe suck the water up and bring that iron ax head to the top when it made its big splash.

- Elisha went over and cut a branch and pointed that branch right where the iron ax head fell into the water and stirred it around, trying to make a tornado-like vortex, and creating a spinning, centrifugal-force action that would cause that iron ax head to come to the top when he stirred the water up.

What it says is this, "He took a stick and threw it into the water." How simple. You've no doubt at some time in your life thrown a stick into a pond or a lake or a river. What does it do? It just creates little ripples.

An important note here:

- There are times in your ministry (but not very many) when what is required of you is to make a big splash, if you want to see a miracle happen.

- There are times in your ministry (but not very many) when if you want to see a miracle happen in the life of your church, you've got to stir things up.

Most of the time, most of the miracles that happen in the life of a local church, happen when we simply create little ripples of influence. That's called culture. How many times have we seen a good pastor go into a situation and try to stir things up or cause a big splash, only to see the congregation turn on the pastor? Why? Because they had not first properly assessed the current church culture and then had failed to establish a culture from which their exciting new ministry thrust could come.

It is a truism: First we set the culture; and when the culture is set, the little ripples of influence that it creates make miracles happen in the life of the church.

Verse 7: *"Lift it out," he said. Then the man reached out his hand and took it.*

So, it floated to the top and Elisha said to the man, "Lift it out." And the unnamed man reached down and he picked it up and lifted it out. Can there ever be truer words spoken about the life of a church and the miracles that can happen in our ministry? Perhaps the real miracle wasn't when an iron ax head floated, but rather it was when "the man reached out his hand and took it."

The miracle in the life of a church doesn't happen until the lay people reach out and grab it. That's the miracle of ministry. When our lay members are freed up through an empowering culture to reach out and take hold of that iron ax head, when church folk enjoy a culture that allows them to buy in to the mission and ministry direction leaders expect, that's when miracles start to happen. "The man reached out his hand and took it." This is one of the minor miracles of the Bible and one of the great stories in the Bible. For me, it's my Bible story. It's the story that says who I am to my congregation and in my work as a church coach, consultant, and workshop presenter.

Incidentally, even though that story ends, Elisha's story doesn't end there. He does other minor miracles. As a matter of fact, Elisha's story continued even beyond his death. You have to get the rest of the story way over in 2 Kings 13:21.

Elisha had long since died. He had been buried and his bones lay forgotten in a tomb at the bottom of a sand dune.

One day, a couple of Israelite men were searching the desert looking for a fitting place to bury the corpse of their recently deceased friend. While they were about their task, they saw in the distance some marauding warriors who seasonally terrorized the inhabitants. Not wanting to be captured and not wanting the marauders to defile the body of their friend, they threw the corpse down a sand dune. The body rolled down the dune and ended up hitting Elisha's tomb.

Well here, let me share how the Scriptures tell it: *"So they threw the man's body into Elisha's tomb. When the body touched Elisha's bones, the man came to life and stood up on his feet"* (NIV).

That's why I stand in awe of you who are in ministry as lay or clergy in the local church. Because my guess is that someday, long after you are dead and buried and forgotten, some poor woman will go through a terrible divorce or maybe a situation of abuse, struggling with a little kid or teenager, thinking that there is no hope and that she is as good as dead.

She is going to stumble into some church like yours, and she is going to touch the bones of your ministry, what your work has left behind—a blessed children's program, a women's ministry, a healthy culture—and she is going to come back to life. (This imaginary woman is just an example of how your church helps more people in deeper ways than most people can imagine.)

And I believe up in heaven, God's going to smile and Jesus is going to look over at you and say, "See, it was worth it, all that work. All that stress.

75

All that struggle. All those frustrations. So, you weren't ever the big shot in a big church or a bishop or somebody extra special in your denomination or network. It was still worth it. See, those hours you put in and struggle dealing with difficult people and difficult situations and difficult circumstances, it was worth it."

Because it's worth it, we owe it to ourselves, to our people, to our Lord to be the very best clergy and lay people we can be. It's worth it, the effort we put into creating the strongest, clearest culture we can. Amen!

I love that story and I love watching pastors in our workshops come up with their own biblical story upon which they build their church's culture. By this point, you are still in your retreat and reflection time. You have (a) put together a first list of culture words, and (b) drilled down into a biblical story that can show your culture. This third step is by all means necessary. Without it, you can easily become dictatorial or at least look foolish.

The third step is to run your newly found culture words honestly and humbly through close family, friends, associates, and church leaders. You are not asking their permission to begin messaging these words in a strategic way (see the "Show It" phase in the next section). But you are asking if these words truly match who you really are *from their perspective*. Why? Because if you come back with words that would be laughed at by those who know you, they'll say, "What are you smoking? That's nothing like you!" This kind of response probably means you focused on your aspirational you, not the authentic you. If I did the exercise today and came back with words such as *fast*, *daring*, and *glitzy*, that probably means I was unconsciously trying to be like my Harley-riding colleague, Jim Chandler. Believe me, people who know me would guffaw at the thought. Remember, Jesus called his first disciples to go on a fishing trip not a "wishing trip." Be sure your culture words are the real you, not the you that you wish you were.

Culture travels on words. Follow our process but remember to verify what seems to emerge as your words with those who know you closely. That's why we say not to rush this exercise; sometimes and for some pastors it can take a long time. But it's time well spent.

We don't want to imply that our process is the only way to "see it." There are a multitude of ways. For instance, Pastor Josh Howerton, a popular speaker on church culture in the nondenominational world, shared his way of "seeing it" in the most recent Culture Conference 2023 session, "How to Build and Guard a Culture from the Ground Up." For his church (Lakepointe Church) to get over some culture unclarity, leaders approached it with the conviction that culture didn't need to be created, but rather discovered from already existing behaviors—"more like excavation than construction." Josh summarizes the process his church utilizes like this: (1) Define it. One of their catchphrases is, "You can't hit a target you have not drawn." Get clear one what you want to see. (2) How to discover the already existing best behaviors that can form the intentional culture they want to create while stressing that the "culture you create is more important than the vision you cast": He asked six highest-level employees: What five other staffers exhibit behaviors that we want to embody as our culture? Then he asked, "What behavioral common denominators do they appear to share? (3) Once they landed on those common denominators, leadership discovered the culture they wanted to convey. What they discovered about the attitudes of their best staffers was that all of them displayed these common characteristics: (1) They openly and consistently showed their love of Jesus; (2) they honor up, down, and all around throughout the life and personnel of the church; (3) they make it fun; and (4) they "love the church, whatever it takes."

That is Josh's way. Finding your culture words is our way. What way works for you? If neither works for you, we hope this section inspires you to come up with your own intentional way to see the culture you want your church to have. Remember the reason to "see it" is to message your culture words strategically and systematically to your staff, key leaders, leadership and volunteers, and throughout the whole congregation. That's how you create culture.

The word *create* is used here not like *ex nihilo*, like God creating something out of nothing. It is more like bringing cosmos out of chaos or creating possibilities, creating momentum, creating a movement. It is like taking the elements of what is there and bringing them to reality. My mother could make the best cherry pie in the world. She created a masterpiece every time she baked. It wasn't that she created something out of nothing, but rather that she had a unique ability to take existing ingredients and blend them together to create a feast.

The culture you are creating isn't necessarily something totally new, as though through magic you are able to make an incredible something out of nothing. Rather, you blend the ingredients of vision, mission, and purpose with the church's personality, possibilities, and experience in a way that propels the church forward. But first, you have to "See It," that is, the current reality plus your desired results.

An amazing uniqueness to any healthy organizational culture is that while it springs from the leader, the more it becomes embedded throughout the organization (church), the more it becomes owned by the people involved; their attitudes, actions, beliefs, and buy-in not only maintain the culture but also continue to create it. In time, the culture becomes "ours" and the culture becomes more primary than the leader in charge for a season. So remember leaders, you are not arbitrarily inventing a culture to which all employees and members of the church are to be ruthlessly subject. You are creating something that intentionally involves most of the people most of the time as rigorous participants.

The organization (church) needs the leader to speak passionately and often about the "culture" of the church. The church needs to have leadership that is or is becoming clear about their leader's personal culture and how it informs the church's culture.[4]

To summarize, keep in mind the three Bs of discovering your culture words:

- "Be still and know" (*Let God speak in deep listening)* (Psalm 46:10, NIV)
- Biblical (*When your story speaks to others, it may be God talking*)
- Bounce (*your words off trusted friends; it's okay to revise*)

So, if our way of finding your culture words doesn't work for you, what does work? You can be creative, and you must be intentional. One last word on "seeing it." Seeing it requires looking honestly at your current culture and looking deeply into your soul to find and own your culture words. Looking inward is critical but can also be fatal if it leads to becoming inwardly focused, about which we will say more in Part 3. That is to say, be cautious about becoming comfortable looking in. To be effective in ministry requires creating an outwardly focused culture. So be sure to look *at* the needs of the congregants you are serving; look *out* at the community around you to see how your church can serve; look *up* at the Living Lord to see what God is calling you to do.

There is an old adage in the business world that applies to the church world: "If you see the world through Sally Jones's eyes, you'll make the products Sally Jones buys." Just remember that looking inward is the starting point of a ministry that soon looks outward at the world through the eyes of others.

Chapter 9

Say It: Threading Your Culture Words

Even if you have not identified your culture, others have.
—Robert Lewis and Wayne Cordeiro, *Culture Shift*

The "It" in the "See It" phase referred to the culture words—authentic to you as the pastor and confirmed by your key leaders—that will enable the church to achieve its desired results in a particular season of its life. The reason to see it is to develop the messaging vehicle to thread, spread, and embed your culture words throughout the entire congregation. Miss a step, and misfortune will follow.

We are now ready to explore the "Say It" phase. (See diagram #6) Once you truly "see it," now you must "say it," threading the culture words through staff and key leaders, weaving them into a tight-knit team. This must be done before you move to spread and embed the desired culture in a positive and compelling way. Recall how I discovered my culture words: *creative*, *passionate*, and *relevant*. Throughout the remainder of this book, as an example, we will share ways to say those words repeatedly, strategically, and intentionally to create the culture of the church. It requires being intentional about saying them over and over again.

In "Say It," *it* means your culture words that will form the nucleus of the culture you and your church are called to create. Say it repeatedly, passionately, creatively, strategically, intentionally, and naturally. There is a sequence to follow to gain the deepest buy-in:

(1) **Say it first to staff**: Whether your staff consists of one part-time person or forty full-time professionals, say it regularly; teach staff about your culture words through your biblical story. There is a reason Jesus selected a small group from his disciples and went higher up into the hills to teach them and pray with them. Your staff are (or should be) the closest to you and they are the ones who will be the primary culture carriers. Sometimes staff are the weakest link in creating a church's culture and that causes any church to suffer. Thread your culture words through the staff to knit together a unified team.

For instance, strategically throughout the year preach sermons based on your biblical story. Come up with a Bible study that succinctly lifts up your story and sets the stage for culture assessment and change, which you will teach your staff and then key leaders. Say it when orienting new volunteers and dedicated church servants beginning their term of office. Say it when interviewing new staff.

(2) **Say it to key leaders in the church,** once you are confident that staff are getting it. Say it in informal settings like lunch or coffee; say it in targeted meeting settings; say it in one-on-one venues. Try it out with them; teach it to them; begin to build the desire to strengthen the church's culture around and through the church's key leadership. Regardless of the size of your church or your lay leadership structure, if key leaders fail to see it, they will never be able to say it to others, and the church will stall out and cause the culture to stagnate.

(3) **Say it to potential new hires**. As experienced leaders know, the culture fit is more important than a candidate's skill set or even experience. Include in the hiring process ways to share with a candidate your culture words and to assess a candidate for your cultural fit. For instance (using my culture words only as an example), when interviewing a potential hire, I would say it simply: "Here at this church, when it comes to our ministry team, we see ourselves as being creative, passionate, and culturally relevant. Tell me, when you hear that, what comes to mind?" Wait for answers. Then, "Can you share examples of how each of those high values fits into your life?" Then I would share the entire Bible story of Elisha. Afterward I would

say, "Is this story something you resonate with? Could you see it in your life? In your job here?"

The reason most church culture books concentrate on the paid staff is that your staff is absolutely critical to creating and maintaining a great culture. It is not an overstatement to say that often hiring new employees makes or breaks your church's ministry. The inverse is true: have the courage and wisdom to fire any employee who after diligent coaching still does not express your church's cultural values. It only takes one negative employee to turn a good thing sour. As my grandfather used to say, "One bad apple spoils the entire bushel."

A good guide to follow in hiring decisions centers around the three Cs:

- Competency
- Character
- Culture

Competency includes skill set, training, experience, and passion for the job and for the church; character requires background checks and your gut feeling in assessing the candidate. Many churches have learned the hard way that a new employee who looks perfect can torpedo the whole church if the employee reveals any kind of serious character defect. Culture asks the question, "Does this person fit into or with our culture?" And it begs the larger question: "Fit in with what?" When the organizational culture is not clear, hiring a good fit is hit or miss at best. This is, in fact, what happens to so many churches: people are hired, decisions are made, ministry is attempted, but without any intentional alignment with the church's culture because the culture is not clear or definable. The result is a spinning of the wheels, lack of momentum and morale, and sometimes worse.

The following diagram demonstrates how culture moves from leadership through the entire congregation in an intentional and strategic way:

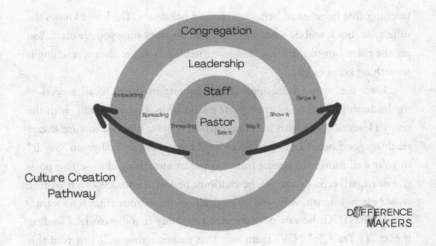

Culture Creation
Pathway

(4) Say it to current lay leadership in your church's structure. And even more importantly for the long-term future, say it to all newly elected/appointed lay leaders throughout the structure. Follow the same process in (3) above and tailor it to fit those wonderful volunteers who make up the heart of your congregation. But good-hearted volunteers can also unwittingly torpedo the church's ministry when—even though they may be good workers—they do not reflect and promote the church's culture.

Most of the time, when staff and volunteers do not or are not able to reflect and promote the church's culture, it is simply the lack of training on leadership's part. But sometimes a church's culture can become toxic when those tasked with servant roles in the church actually operate in undermining ways contrary to the desired culture. The "Say It" phase has a narrow target, and that target is to say it to selected participants in ways that inform, teach, inspire, and motivate.

After many years pastoring in inner-city mission churches, I was appointed to a fast-growing community north of Dallas. The church was in the middle of ranching country, so I did what any pastor would do: I learned to ride horses. Roy, the old rancher who mentored me, used to say, "When you get on a good horse for the first time, that horse knows you are new. Your ride is never neutral. Every time you get in the saddle, you are teaching that horse good behaviors, or bad behaviors. The horse knows the difference, but it will do what you train it to do every time you are on it. You are the rider, but to the horse it is never neutral. You are always teaching it something good or bad."

Over the years I have applied that equestrian lesson to all aspects of my leadership. As senior pastor, your relationship with your staff, with the church leadership, or with the congregation is never neutral! You are always teaching good behavior or bad behavior. How, when, and why you "Say It" to your staff moves the needle from neutral to something else—either positive or negative. So be careful; be cautious; be courageous. Say your culture words often, intentionally, and strategically to move your church forward.

WARNING: Beware of speaking to anybody in a dictatorial, "lording it over" (1 Peter 5:3 NIV) them way that comes across as "I just read this book and learned how to change our culture." But rather proceed in an inviting, positive way, such as: "I love pastoring this church when I see people being creative with their gifts, and I look forward to being with you as we find ways to strengthen and build upon that."

Of course when we talk about "saying it," we urge you to anchor the "it" in your personal culture words, but certainly don't limit what you say to those three or four words. You will sound like an automaton! And not very in tune with your own people. A good practice for threading the culture throughout the staff and leaders is to be verbal and vocal and intentional in praising people consistently! In *Habits of Healthy Churches*, Marcus Carlson reminds us that:

> Behavior that gets celebrated gets repeated. Consistently affirm the practice of values as they unfold in your church. Here are some ideas to help celebrate your values: (a) Privately and publicly affirm those who model the values; (b) reward behaviors that are consistent with values; (c) highlight testimonials and stories that that reinforce values during weekend worship—videos, messages, etc. (d) Give team members opportunities to share "wins" during meetings and gatherings; (e) Connect wins to the church values; (f) elevate values during marker moment celebrations.[1]

One last word about culture words before we move on. We are often asked, "Should other staff members do their own personal 'finding your culture words' exercise?" We have found that perhaps for their own interest they may go through it; but if a church tries to convey too many culture words, the culture becomes foggy, mushy, or otherwise unfocused. It is far better to create the culture based on the senior pastor's words and the leadership's affirmation; then the staff learns, understands, accepts, and buys into those words by saying it throughout their circles of influence. As the senior pastor and staff continue to say it, the culture begins to take hold and moves into the "Show It" phase throughout the leadership and into the congregation.

In the "Show It" phase detailed in the next chapter we share specific practices designed to spread the culture throughout the congregation.

Before we get there, however, try this intentional exercise for staff and key leaders to bridge between "saying it" (threading) and "showing it" (spreading): Incorporate and build from the short, pocket-sized book, *Five Marks of a Methodist*, by Steve Harper.[2] Make it a team reading and processing assignment for staff and key leaders to do together. But don't just read it. Use it as a guide for the team to begin intentionally identifying—and writing out—what you would call, "Five Marks of Our Culture." Notice the simplicity of Steve's five marks: (1) A Methodist Loves God; (2) A Methodist Rejoices in God; (3) A Methodist Gives Thanks; (4) A Methodist Prays Constantly; (5) A Methodist Loves Others. Steve points out that all of these come from John Wesley's document, "The Character of a Methodist."

Write your document out as a team; struggle with it; live with it, and be sure to identify it as a draft that will be worked on by more and more people as the culture spreads through the congregation. An added value to using Steve Harper's book: It will help you be sure the values upon which your culture is built are compatible with Methodism's! Even for non-Methodists, this kind of exercise using foundational documents for your respective denominations can be a great help to get to clarity and to begin writing out the values which shape your culture.

With this exercise as a bridge, let's move on to spreading the culture through the church.

Chapter 10

Show It: Spreading Your Culture Words

In any culture where we function, and especially where we have influence,
we either foster toxicity or health.
—Marcus J. Carlson, *Habits of Healthy Churches*

The word *It* in the "Show It" phase is the culture of the church that now emanates from the pastor and staff as a close-knit unified team working together for the good of the church and for the sake of the gospel. You have begun to "Say It"—your culture words which are a vehicle to carry the culture—but while you are saying over and over again those three or four memorable words you must also contextualize those words within the expressed values that you and the church manifest. It is integral to the process to define your values regularly from the platform through study opportunities, in casual hallway conversations, and even in governance settings. Not just you, but staff and key leaders as well. And, as Kevin Gerald reminds us, "In defining your values, be careful where your heart is. The Bible teaches us that our heart will pursue whatever we treasure: 'For where your treasure is, there your heart will be also' (Matthew 6:21). In designing a church culture, stating what we value gives team members an opportunity to put their hearts into the tasks that uphold those treasures."[1]

This phase moves toward an increasingly wide target audience, and the approach is to make the culture visible and tangible in all aspects of the church's life. The way to do this is to show it in and through:

- worship
- hallway talk (hospitality vignettes), visuals, and the feel of the place
- meetings
- healthy feedback systems

Obviously, the "Show It" phase is still "saying it" but often in ways other than verbal and more tangible for wider buy-in . As we alluded to in the previous chapter, the culture words you have identified and that you say over and over again to staff and key leaders are the vehicles to communicate the values and desired culture. In this chapter you will see how those same words continue to serve as the vehicle to spread the culture now beyond the staff and into the wider congregation. The best way to do this is to leverage those culture words to "show" the desired culture so that others can grasp it, and buy in to it. You will be showing much more than those culture words, and where and the ways you show those words will convey the key elements of your culture.

Edgar Schein identified key elements of any culture that can be shown with intentionality and that carry the leading values of the organization: "Rites, rituals, physical space; stories about events and people; formal statements, philosophy, creeds and charters."[2] More recently, Lovett Weems, in addressing the church-specific culture, wrote that the culture spreads throughout the church through the following ways: language, space, symbols, rituals, heroes, recognitions, daily routines, and cultural networks.[3]

Showing it becomes a more intentional step to build upon the effort of threading the culture words throughout the staff; now the intent is to spread those words throughout the leaders and influencers in the church. It is the "spreading" phase that paves the way for change, because it leads to buy-in. Take for example the "rituals" of your church—not just those on Sunday morning, but throughout the week in all sorts of ways that bond people together. I personally experienced the power of healthy rituals as a way to spread the culture throughout an expanding congregation when I followed a very popular planting pastor, Bill Jacobs, at Trietsch Memorial UMC. The church had developed a number of positive healthy rituals to bond people together and allowed for its remarkable growth. One was their self-identify as "Trietscher Creatures." Trietsch (pronounced as "to reach" said quickly) had an amazing capacity to include new people quickly as they bought in to becoming a "Trietscher creature." Prior to planting the church Bill had served as an Air Force chaplain; he knew the importance of this and how to bond people together quickly around tradition and rituals. It was a joy for me when I went beyond being their pastor to becoming a Trietscher Creature myself!

Included in this "spreading" phase are hints of how to make visible and tangible the culture throughout the congregation and to paint a picture of the cultural values and behaviors you hope to see in your church, much like Jesus did when he taught the Beatitudes.

Jesus was not only demonstrating a deep spiritual yearning but also showing what it looked like to be a part of his sacred community of believers and to paint a picture of the culture that would bind his followers together. Throughout the New Testament we see countless other examples of Jesus showing his followers and the world the culture that would change the world. "See how they loved each other," wrote the ancient historian Tertullian, because Jesus created a movement whose very culture was to "Love one another" (John 13:34), and it was a culture so clearly lived out that anyone could see it because adherents would show it in their lives and in their relationships. Here are some key places to show it in your church.

Show It in Worship

We don't claim to be preaching coaches, but in our experience many preachers have focused on "proclaiming the Word of God"—which no doubt is the primary purpose of a sermon—to the exclusion of intentionally taking the opportunity of creating the culture of their church during the worship service. Here are a few tested hints to create culture in worship without distracting from praising God:

(1) Make sure that the worship (or at least parts of it) is intentionally interactive and engaging. I don't mean engaging in the sense of interesting (hopefully the message and the entire service will be that) but in a way that

is intentionally interactive with the people who are there or who are worshipping online.

Responsive readings of Scripture or call to worship or other litanies served the function of interaction and engagement for generations, and served well. But today. Not so much for many audiences. The culture in which most people live has catapulted interaction and engagement into a whole new sphere, as evidenced by technology, popular television, and entertainment venues. Wherever people go, they are enmeshed in a ramped-up world of interaction and engagement: The "kiss cam" at a professional sporting events isn't designed simply to be entertaining; it is interactive and engaging. *Please note: We are not suggesting stopping liturgies; but just examine if it might elevate your worship experience to add other interactive elements.*

It will be increasingly difficult to speak the language of today's emerging generations in worship if we aren't intentional about finding creative ways for people to be actively engaged. This engagement may be a special feature of the service or ongoing use of social media or texting or a style of communicating. What books, podcasts, and online publications are you and your team studying that keep up with newer technologies like AI? If nothing else, try something similar to what we first wrote about in *Clip In* (Abingdon, 2014). Have the final slide on your screens at the conclusion of the worship time, read simply: "If you have questions about anything you heard or experienced today, text #_____ and one of our staff will get back to you within two hours." (If you don't use screens, print the message in your Worship Guide.) Be sure that you have a dedicated cell phone number that can be rotated among staff of key laity to field any inquiries, and be diligent to provide immediate response.

This simple message tells attenders—especially those in the 18-to 40-year-old range—that you speak their language: thumb! Even if you never get a texted question, you are communicating your desired culture of a connecting, engaging, "it's about you" experience.

When you do get a texted question or comment, your response may open the way for greater connection or conversation that may well lead to a church relationship or even a personal friendship.

As a bonus, you've gotten a cell phone number. Keep a database of all cell numbers; and when you are publicizing events—especially hands-on, serving opportunities—send out "blast texts" to all the numbers. This can prove to be a quick and easy way to communicate in relevant fashion with many people who will never read the church bulletin or other written appeals.

(2) Connecting: We discussed previously the phenomenon that "culture travels on words, so be sure that the words spoken from the platform, and that appear on screens and bulletins or worship guides, are carefully thought out with intentionality to connect and create culture. Avoid distancing words creating a non-intended chasm between the already-connected and the not-yet-connected. Avoid things like "join us for _____." Instead, focus on the *benefits* available to anyone who participates in that event: "Great fun for families!"

Here's why: *Join us* are two words that create suspicion in the minds of critical first-time attenders. *Join*—they aren't ready to join anything and certainly do not want to be considered as "fresh meat" that the church is trying to recruit for its purposes.

Us is different from *them* and distances the guest from the church. *They* are not part of the *us*—will they be valued if they don't become part of the *us*? Is the agenda to help them, meet their needs, serve them, engage them, provide them outlets to serve; or is the agenda to get them to become part of us? It sounds like, "It's all about us!" "Join us!" More crassly, this language is institution oriented: become part of the institution. It is less about meeting people where they are. It's just not as pleasant to the person who is not already or at least not particularly inclined to want to become part of the "us." They may be attending for the first time simply out of some personal need they hope gets addressed.

Here is a simple reminder summary:

- Connecting words *("You'll love this!")*

- Distancing words *("Join us.")*

- Model camaraderie on platform (*have fun with each other*)

Also, actively engage people in ways to become producers of the ministry. It's okay to create expectation: "If you are a first time guest, you are probably here for more than just hearing what we have to say; you are looking for a place and way to make a difference. So, I invite you to check out how you can do something really helpful at the church's Habitat House build, or in collecting food for the hungry," and so on. This helps first-timers see immediate ways to connect with a cause or a purpose. More important, they see that your deepest desire for them to connect is more meaningful than institutional—it is missional. Be invitational in getting people connected and involved. Provide specifics of how people can put into practice what you are talking about, and share on screens videos highlighting real-life stories of people actually doing it! My friend Jason Moore, one of the best worship and hospitality practitioners in the country, says it like this: "Don't let your screens just be bulletins on the wall; screens are for telling a story."

Remember Elisha's story, "The man reached out his hand and took it." When laity "reach out and take it," this creates a culture that unleashes them to model to other laity what it means to be a disciple. Laity often can motivate other laity better than the clergy can.

(3) Actively engage the congregation in sermon planning. Line out themes far in advance and publicize topics. Solicit emails, texts, and Facebook comments that share stories that you may want to use in your message. Their story may help shape someone else's story. This is relational! It is hospitable! It's engaging! It's connecting! It's friendly!

The pastor of a struggling church we worked with in Florida decided to put this principle into practice. He and his worship team figured out they could leverage the unfortunate growth of toxic algae along the beach that had the attention of the whole community. They developed a sermon series, "Toxic Relationships." Not only did the title create a relevant connection, but also he promoted the series well in advance and solicited real-life stories from people about relationships gone bad. Some of the stories they received he used in his series. But he wisely responded to everyone who shared a story, even if their story did not appear in worship, which strengthened relationships. They lined up speakers and special programs designed to help people going through all sorts of toxic relationships. Attendance for the series skyrocketed, but the lasting impact was the culture it created within the church: a culture that valued story, relationship, relevance, connection, creativity, and intentionality. Today, that church has moved beyond crisis mode and is growing in health and vitality.

(4) Model a spirit of camaraderie, teamwork, and having fun on the platform. What happens when first-time guests see and experience elaborate hospitality with great buzz and laughter and an effervescent spirit when they walk in? It connects with them. Now imagine what happens when what they see and experience during the worship service has a totally different feel; when it seems rote, staid, and mechanical, even if it is done with great dignity and efficiency and even when all the individual parts of the service—such as the sermon and the music—are done well. If the feel of the worship service does not match the feel of the hospitality they've experienced in the hallways, there is a disconnect.

It is the disconnect that shakes the culture and makes it difficult for first-time guests to smoothly navigate through the experience we want them to have. Faster growing nondenominational churches have grasped the importance of being sure that the hospitality *around* the worship service matches the hospitality *in* the worship service. That is a key to creating a *culture* of hospitality.

Show It in Hallway Talk

Your church's culture is generally demonstrated in its hospitality. Without showing your congregation a healthy, strong, clear, irresistible culture, your church will either crash or spin its wheels, getting little traction in the highly competitive church world of today. Showing it constantly reminds staff, leadership, the congregation, and the community of what your church values and how it goes about doing its ministry. Showing it requires the culture (especially your culture and systems of hospitality) to be: (1) clearly taught; (2) constantly modeled; (3) consistently practiced; and (4) widely prioritized.

Reminder! As we alluded to earlier, none of the above four behaviors can be successfully accomplished without good systems in place. Here is a truism worth remembering: Good Systems without Clear Culture = Activity. But: Clear Culture without Good System = Spinning your wheels on the slippery road of good intentions and wishful thinking.

Pop icon Taylor Swift's Eras Tour was the music sensation of the year. But it became mired in controversy when the ticket outlet company, Ticketmaster, crashed because it failed to anticipate the popularity of the event and didn't have systems in place to keep up with ticket demand. So it is with your church system: if your systems can't deliver or fail to meet the needs of the church, bad things will happen. Churches flounder when they self-perceive to have a strong culture but have weak systems to carry out their ministry.

Your church's culture is the key expression of "the feel of the place." Have you ever had the experience of going into a new place like a restaurant, a school, a business, or even a church and you can just feel the vibes of the place? First-time guests often get this gut-level feeling when they come into your church or even onto your property. How the place looks in terms of sharpness and cleanliness certainly contributes to this feeling but is not all of it. How people interact with one another; how signage anticipates your questions; how a spirit of kindness, joy, fun, hospitality, and thoughtfulness just seems so evident! This is the result of culture.

Leaders tend to agree on the practice of "over communicating" to get information out to inform the congregation about important events. We agree, but there's a warning. It is easy to over communicate information when what truly needs to be communicated is the "why" behind the "what." An example: In the announcement time, someone from the podium highlights a mission-critical emphasis like this: "Next Sunday we will be collecting men's new underwear for the homeless shelter; leave your donation in the box outside the sanctuary."

This is needed and motivational *information (the "what")*, but culture is created when you equally emphasize "why." So simply add: "This is why we exist, to help others in need." Say it over and over; over communicate the "why" as much as the "what." That's what gets the attention of the first-time guest. Or add to that announcement something like this: "That's what so many people say they love about this church. That so many people jump in to help in so many ways." Remember—culture travels on words. Be strategic and intentional to include the "why" whenever a "what" is mentioned. It may seem unimportant at first and it is easy to unwittingly become a church of "whats." In the end, you will, as they say, "be preaching to the choir." But once you get used to it, you'll find it's easy to include the "why" and you will have a much improved chance of reaching a first-time guests and creating a culture that makes them want to return.

When it comes to creating culture, you intentionally "Show It" because the better you show it, the easier it is to communicate your identity. Your culture sets your identity. A clearly understood identity is not only important, it is critical to effectiveness in the ministry world today. Identity— what most people, most of the time say when talking about your church— is important! What they are saying reveals the community's perception of your culture. But it is not easy to create and maintain the kind of culture that identifies your church to those who are not yet a part of it. There are constant pressures from all sorts of places, internally and externally, that distract the church from being who it authentically is. The church can become so busy in the weeds of ministry that it takes for granted that everybody in the congregation and in the community knows who it is, leading to the church forgetting to constantly and creatively message its identity. Having a clearly felt identity is a critical step in allowing the church to create the culture it chooses to message. Remaining intentional about reminding itself and fortifying its identity is just as important.What creates culture in ways that establish identity in any organization is when there is consistency of messaging throughout the organization. Healthy culture is when "who you say you are" matches "how you do what you do." It happens when "what you do" and "what you say you do" and "why you do it" connect with and reflect the hearts and passions of others. Culture happens when—from top to bottom throughout every tentacle of the organization—there is clarity and consistency of messaging, behavior, attitude, and actions. It is critical that the spirit of what happens *in* worship matches what happens *around* worship. Otherwise, you may be doing some good things but hardly creating a culture that connects. How to do this? Make sure the elements of every worship experience include the key key components of healthy culture: intentional, relational, interactive, engaging, and connecting.

Show It in Visuals

What artwork, displays, communications, and messaging is visually seen on walls, desks, and in gathering spaces? What does it say about you? To guests? How does it remind staff and key leaders of taking responsibility for the culture of the church? Is it creative and compelling?

Recently I set out to replace a cracked windshield in our Honda CRV. The first place we went to was supposedly the industry's largest and its heavy marketing got our attention. But our visit was less than satisfying: they made mistakes on scheduling, were misleading on availability of the right windshield, and made us wait in a cramped, dingy waiting room . The walls and the hallways were covered in further marketing info and industry publications bragging about their service.

So we kept looking and spoke to someone who suggested a lesser-known shop, and not nearly as convenient to get to as the first place we tried, but in their words: "We had an absolutely great experience there and will never go anywhere else." So based on their recommendation, we decided to give it a try. From our very first phone call to when I drove the car out of the shop, it was a pleasing encounter! Here's why:

The owners, Paula and Jack, provided an unmatched approach to keeping existing customers happy and to rely upon word-of-mouth referrals instead of putting budget money into mass marketing. We enjoyed having the choice of two spacious, well-adorned waiting areas with outstanding hospitality. Every employee was well trained in customer service and genuinely messaged how much they loved working there.

Instead of the usual constant barrage of upselling posters stuck on the walls and tables, their visuals were totally different; they expressed creativity, values, and fun. Their commercially bought signage had nothing directly to do with their business, but it had everything to do with their culture. The wall art said nothing about "what they do" but said plenty about "how they go about doing what they do."

Churches would be wise to post in their hallways something similar. Banners and artwork of specifically spiritual/religious themes are okay, but that is what they do; show the culture in how you go about doing what you do. This culture art has a dual purpose: it tells customers a little about who they are, and more important it constantly reminds every employee of their shared values. As one young employee told me, "I walk through here dozens of times every day, and every time I am reminded of how I am supposed to act as a team member."

Too often a first-time guest to a church walks into the long hallway filled with pictures of all the previous pastors, of when the scouts went to a jamboree in 1952, of the quilt Aunt Lucille donated to a fundraiser in 1968. You get the picture (no pun intended). Actually, none of those are inherently bad or inappropriate, but a good rule of thumb is for every picture of past glory days, just add colorful, creative pictures of the present and a compelling future. I am not saying to take down pictures from the past, which may rightfully offend parishioners, but intentionally balance out the past with the present and future. If you happen to be in one of those facilities that is showing its age, spruce up hallways with smiling photos of children. Big, easy-to-see, smiling pictures. Be sure there are big pictures of church people in mission, working together while having fun. Take a small group of leaders through the facility to look specifically at anything that might be perceived by a first-time guest as negative. Then find something positive to put near it. It is great to see artwork of eye-catching places in your community, to which first-time guests can relate. Another rule of thumb is before you try to get the church to go out into the mission field, find ways to bring the mission field into the church. So we ask again: What artwork, displays, communications, and messaging is visually seen on walls, desks, and in gathering spaces at your church? What does it say about you? To guests? How does it remind staff and key leaders of taking responsibility for the culture of the church?

Show It in Meetings

Regardless of the size of your church or the size of your staff, your church is going to hold meetings. Aspirationally viewed as holy conversations, but more realistically seen as committees or boards or teams conducting the business of the church. Most people in church will shrug meetings off as anything from a necessary evil to a waste of time. And yet we must hold our meetings. We are not here to urge churches to avoid or do away with meetings, but we do hope to make the case that in addition to conducting business, a church's meetings are a great place to show the culture of the church. Why not turn meetings into an event that shows the culture of the church to participants, reminding them constantly of the importance of maintaining a strong, healthy culture?

The following is a sad but true story that almost every pastor of a mainline church has experienced: A good friend and member just seems to stop showing up. You wonder why. He and his wife are generous and supportive; they have chaired nearly every committee the church has, often more than once. At first you assume they have been traveling or ill or busier than usual. But then gradually it becomes apparent they are no longer active in church. Finally you figure out how to have a conversation with them. "Pastor," he says, "We love you and the church, but we are just burned out." Then his wife chimes in, "Honestly, we just no longer are feeling fed here."

This exchange is deflating to any pastor. But here is what the pastor didn't know: his good members did truly experience burnout because most of their church time was spent in meetings, doing the business of the church, as loyal members often do. Along the way a friend invites them to a neighborhood Bible study, where they study the Bible, pray, and begin to experience Christian community in which they feel "fed." They didn't even know the neighborhood Bible study was actually sponsored by the megachurch around the corner; the megachurch's Bible study groups gather together for a celebration service at the end of the Bible study season, and it is powerful with personal testimonies by people in similar Bible studies. The worship feels good; they feel fed. And as they form more connections, they start to attend the megachurch and become staunch supporters, leaving your church behind.

This little vignette portays a part of many independent megachurches growth strategy. Their target audience goes well beyond unchurched "lost souls" but mostly appeals to dissatisfied mainline church members who describe themselves as burned out, unfed, and unhappy.

Let's break this down: Meetings and the endless menu of good things for any member to help out with are a major cause of burnout. People have limited time and the amount of time they allocate to their church is getting shorter and shorter. So when the members evaluate their involvement in church and it dawns on them that mainly they are going to meetings, it takes a toll. Good church folk understandably want to make a difference in their world, and to do that they seek out opportunities for hands-on ministry. All too often they end up going to meetings instead. In the short term, they are happy to help; in the long term, they suffer burnout.

Keeping in mind the time limitations that most people have today, become ultra intentional to turn your meetings into more than conducting business. Let your meetings become a setting where people are fed, where they feel like their time spent was worthwhile, and where the culture of the church is maintained and reflected. It is really easy to transform meetings, but it does take intentionality and a commitment to constantly show the culture of the church as a reminder of "who we are" and "how we go about doing things around here." Following are some good hints and helpful tools that can transform any meeting, including decision-making meetings of key lay leaders, support meetings of volunteers in a particular ministry, and even staff meetings.

For meetings: First, wherever possible, publish in handout form or digitally the agenda of the meeting, beginning with something like this statement of purpose: "To conduct business while at the same time using our time together for spiritual growth and support, and to continuously proclaim our culture of what it means to be a *creative, culturally relevant, passionate church* as part of our DNA" (substitute your own culture words as developed from the "See It" phase of creating culture).

Second, welcome all participants by directly connecting selected persons to how they exemplify or reflect the culture of the church. ("So glad, Stella, to see you here tonight. I just love the way you show our culture of support and love in everything you do!") This not only builds up people, but also casts the vision and highlights some aspect of the culture of the church.

Third, be intentional about creating an environment of being scripturally fed in every meeting. Here's an example: divide into small groups ("get in groups of three, knee to knee") and do some five- to ten-minute sharing/praying exercises. This creates two important factors for "feeling fed": one, people get to share their story and hear the stories of others; and two, people praying for one another. As an example, in their small groups people share a personal story that ties into something that is current and relevant. For instance, a pastor in Texas shared with me that during early spring flooding in the Houston area, he used that rainfall event to set up this sharing time: "We have all been affected by these terrible floods. So please take turns in your group and share briefly about a time when you were 'flooded with grief or sorrow.'" Stories were shared about the death of a grandparent or friend or other tragedies. It just took three or four minutes to share stories. Then the pastor brought them to the prayer time: "Now, would you take the hand of the person next to you; just pray for the person on your right that they may experience rainbows of hope and assurance, no matter what they may be flooded within life right now. If you are not comfortable praying out loud, just squeeze the hand of the person you are praying for." This simple exercise is powerful and memorable.

Next, use a marker board or other technique that everyone can see. Ask someone to go to the marker board and invite meeting participants to popcorn (quickly and randomly shout out responses) to the entire group regarding the accomplishments they've seen in the respective areas since the last meeting or throughout the year. You will be amazed (and so will your members!) at how much you have done. This should take no more than three to five minutes. People want to make a difference, so set a positive tone early in the meeting.

This introductory time of story sharing, prayer, and accomplishments should only last six to twelve minutes. But we have found that these minutes on the front end of the meeting often save thirty to forty minutes on the back end of the meeting. One reason is that meetings can be difficult sometimes and people can get frustrated with each other. It is much harder for someone to get tacky with someone else after they have prayed together. Meetings also often become opinion heavy. We often hear a lot of "in my opinion" talk. Unfortunately, people seldom have opinions; more often, their opinions have them. The tools we've introduced aim to help a meeting become more about discernment than opinion.

This cultural intentionality works well for sixty to ninety minutes for a meeting. Any more time is ineffective, so please respect the schedules of your members. In the meantime, meetings will become a valuable place to show the culture and to create an environment in which participants share stories and pray for one another—where everyone feels fed while doing the business of the church.

Positive traction forward happens when the church's culture is well-known and is clearly seen as the launchpad of everything the church does. Regardless of the size of your church or staff, most churches stumble, spin their wheels, and lose vitality when the church becomes "thing oriented" instead of "culture motivated." One effective way to show the culture is by developing a set of written values by which staff and key leaders serve in their positions. On the next page is an example; use it or let it inspire your own creativity and intentionality to develop something similar. This kind of document should be widely publicized and regularly used in meeting setting

My thanks to the former pastor of Memorial Drive United Methodist Church in Houston, Chuck Simmons, for first sharing this kind of document with me.

BEATITUDES TO SERVE BY
& STRENGTHEN CULTURE

BLESSED ARE YOU who possesses a positive attitude displayed at all times in the presence of members, visitors, and fellow workers, for even small seeds of negativism grow into large weeds.

BLESSED ARE YOU who see your assigned duties as a unique ministry in the Kingdom of God, for those who are dependable in learning and diligently applying their craft bring joy to the household of faith.

BLESSED ARE YOU who let the spirit of teamwork shine at all times, for its light illumines the dark corners of fatigue and discouragement that from time to time may creep in upon us all.

BLESSED ARE YOU who risks creatively changing things for the better, for initiative on behalf of the Lord is more to be desired than the wings of angels.

BLESSED ARE YOU who looks upon all persons with the eyes of Christ, for compassion and understanding are more esteemed than judgmentalism and self-righteousness.

BLESSED ARE YOU who ask, "What can I do to help?" with as much concern as "whose task is it?" for the future is found in the team that works together for the glory of God.

BLESSED ARE YOU who speaks of no problem without offering a solution, for the tongue of the complainer is not as worthy as the lips of a problem solver.

BLESSED ARE YOU who dwell in the abode of humble service with your brothers and sisters rather than wait alone outside the gates of haughty superiority, for there the heart of the servant is found.

BLESSED ARE YOU who find no fault in thy brother or sister that you are unwilling to discuss with them in Christian love, for "talking to" is far mightier than "talking about."

BLESSED ARE YOU whose smile and pleasant disposition are known throughout the church, for a "no" spoken in courtesy is better than a "yes" spoken in contempt.

Show It in Healthy Feedback Systems

Of the multitude of churches we work with regarding their culture, one constant stands out: when a church has a healthy culture, there are healthy feedback systems in place; when a church is struggling, the feedback systems are either not in place or are poorly maintained. Feedback is a safe way for people (staff, leaders, parishioners) to feel like their voice is heard, their concerns acknowledged, and their presence and their contributions valued.

It has long been a practice in organizations that have a good culture to use a practice of the "ten-minute stand up" meeting on a regular basis. This approach may be a helpful practice for you; but if it doesn't feel right, let your creativity and intentionality shine through to come up with predictable, expected ways to truly listen to your team members and congregation and, when needed, to implement fair ways of evaluating events, processes, teams, and staff. Every church is going to have some rough edges and conflict along the way; the best way to deal with it is through good feedback systems.

Chapter 11

Grow It: Embedding Culture in the Congregation

By changing your church's culture, you are releasing its future.
—Robert Lewis and Wayne Cordeiro, *Culture Shift*

To recap, our four-step process began with the "see it," then moved intentionally to "say it," and advanced strategically to "show it" and now in this chapter it accelerates passionately into "grow it." Yes, your church's growth accelerates as your healthy, relevant, compelling culture is truly embedding within the life of the congregation. We say "embedding"—not embedded—because culture is constantly evolving and re-creating itself.

William Vanderbloemen, in *Culture Wins*, cites his alma mater, Texas A&M University and its famous culture: A culture is a way of life of a group of people—the behaviors, beliefs, values, and symbols that they accept, generally without thinking about them, and that are passed along by communication and imitation from one generation to the next.[1]

It is the "passing from one generation to the next" that enables sustained growth in any organization, including your church. It occurs with embedding the desired culture in the church, the culmination of our intentional process to make the culture known, evident, and central to the life of the church. Embedding means that most of the people most of the time demonstrate your desired cultural values. Not everyone will, all the time, but most of the people can, most of the time. When the cultural values are seamlessly and naturally embedding themselves in the life of the church it means that the culture is being transmitted from one person to the next;

103

from one subgroup to the next; from one generation to the next. Without embedding, people will perceive the culture differently. There will be little consistency or identity.

We hear a lot about "creating a culture of growth." But growth is not a kind of culture; it is a result of culture. Culture is made of those little things done repeatedly and well that become "how we go about doing the things we do," unleashing the ability to grow. Church growth (or the lack of it) is a result of your church's culture. Culture is something other than growth, but growth is often the result.

The "it" in the grow phase means the growth of the church. Jesus powered the "Grow It" phase of the New Testament by sending the Holy Spirit at Pentecost. We can't send the Holy Spirit; that's already been done. But we can share some helpful hints to grow your church by creating a healthy culture.[2]

In *Change the Culture, Change the Game,* Roger Connors and Tom Smith rightly point out two truths that are applicable to our work in the church world:

1. The results you are getting are because of the culture you have; if you want to change the results, you have to change the culture.

2. Most organizations grow by reaching people, those people returning to the church and those people recommending the church to others.[3]

The premise of this book is to focus on creating a strong, healthy culture which can help change the results we've been getting in our local churches and denomination. One of those results is to learn how embedding the desired culture helps accelerate our growth by accomplishing the three Rs.

The idea behind creating a strong, healthy culture is to change the results we've been getting in our local churches and denominations We are now at the place where the pastor and leadership must be totally committed to this culture change and creation endeavor! As Yoda famously said to Luke in *Star Wars,* "Do or do not; there is no try." Once committed, employ the following process to put legs under that commitment to accelerate growth by accomplishing the three Rs. Our experience is that churches grow at the pace with which the three Rs occur:

1. Reaching
2. Returning
3. Recommending

These three Rs are what drive churches to get new participants, get them to return, and then get them to recommend the church to others.

Churches—like other organizations that depend upon new customers or new business—must structurally be designed and oriented to excel at all three. I went into the ministry under the amazing missionary/evangelist E. Stanley Jones. He used to say that "the church is not an organization. It is a living organism."

While I agree with the sentiment behind that statement, it is not totally accurate. If there is too much organization, it can stifle the energy of the living organism. But if there is too little or ineffective organization, it can choke the growth of the living organism by turning its activities and movement into a chaotic mess. Truth: The church is both a living organism and an organization. If it is to "the gates of Hades will not prevail against it" (Matt 16:17-19 NRSVUE) it has to incorporate both understandings and to excel at each. It is the organizational culture of the church that allows it to excel at the three Rs.

Reaching. Often, reaching new people is actually the easiest for a church, but it leads only to the first and often lowest tier of growth. Many churches are excited about reaching this tier and then stop; their growth ceases and they simply spin their wheels without going forward. Denominations and church-planting movements have figured out the best way to reach new people is to start a new church. Similarly, within an existing church, the best way to reach new people is to start a new ministry (worship service, hands-on helping initiative, new staff member, etc.). Starting a new ministry is a good opportunity to reach new people who were not previously connected to the church, or perhaps to any church, or even to the gospel.

But it does not always have to be something new. Many churches experience a jump in attendance numbers at special events such as Christmas Eve or Easter services or Mother's Day when they promote heavily in the community with top-notch media blitzes. Sometimes a church will find itself the beneficiary of a new housing development nearby. With just a little prompting, the youth group or some larger group of church parishioners can distribute doorknob hangers and may actually see results the next Sunday. In these cases, it isn't the church that is new; it is the people who are new. And this is a prime time to reach new people. But as stated before, reaching people only results in first-tier growth (whatever the number). It can become counterproductive because sometimes a church attempts repeated similar efforts to reach new people with little success, demoralizing even their best leaders.

Returning. New people are often reached because of the church's efforts to provide something compelling that attracts others to the church and its ministry. But for those people who come for the first time, it is the church's healthy culture that motivates guests to return to check out the church more deeply. The culture brings about the returning effect.

I (Yvette) worked with a pastor who took over a congregation after its founding pastor left following a lengthy tenure. The first Sunday after the pastor left, the attendance dropped from 1,500 at its peak to 350. People warned the incoming lead pastor that attendance would likely decline. Fortunately, that pastor was wise and elected not to focus on attendance (growth) but to focus on making a positive culture shift under his leadership through "See It, Say It, Show It, Grow It." Within one year the attendance was at 1,000 on a Sunday and giving was at levels equal to or greater than the previous year. This new growth included some previous attendees who came back after warming up to the new pastor, but the majority were new people God was drawing into the church because of its clear culture reflected in its faithfulness to John 12:32: "And I, when I am lifted up from the earth, will draw all people to myself" (NIV).

This pastor made the right culture shift. It was what people in the community were seeking and craving and could not find anywhere else. The culture shift created the opportunity for growth *without* a dedicated institu-

106

tional focus specifically on growth. In all that we do in the church, a healthy culture allows good things to happen through our obedience, or merely the miracle of God. With a good marketing campaign, a church can often reach people, but getting those folk to return requires two things. The first thing is a good "product": a worship experience that is worthy of returning to; a church environment that is inviting, welcoming, and relevant. It requires a compelling vision, a missional focus, an attractive physical plant, the quality of childcare, the genuine sense of hospitality, the way the church connects to people. That's the product. The second thing is the pace at which you can get the first-time attendee to become significantly involved in the ministry of the church—to intentionally move them beyond being a consumer to becoming a producer. That is often referred to as "making new disciples."

Getting to the next tier of growth requires that a significant number of the people you've reached will actually return. Given worship attendance trends of late, this return may or may not be the very next Sunday after their initial visit. Often return visits are random and sporadic. But still, getting a sizeable number of people you have reached to return will jump-start the church to second-tier growth (whatever the number for your context).

Don't be dismayed over these trends in worship attendance, even among regular members. Most of us in the church world grew up in a time when a so-called loyal church member attended every Sunday. At worst, they attended three out of four Sundays. But now, most research (and anecdotal evidence) suggests a loyal member today will attend about 1.2 times a month.

Pastors, don't panic. It does not help to berate your congregation on Sunday mornings for more people not being present. This scolding does not go over well and is offensive to the folk who are in fact present. The value of getting people to return is not so much in the number and the frequency of return visits, but in the connectional bond they form.

Getting people to return is about understanding what people are looking for when they come to your church. Your church's culture should be intentional about meeting the needs and expectations of those who are coming, and it should clearly give space for their stories to be heard. Within their stories is the answer to the question, "What do people in our community need?"

For Impact Church, we know that people initially come for the seventy-five-minute worship service, the casual dress, and the dynamic and creative worship experience. Then, as we intentionally connect with them and learn their stories, they stay for the opportunities to relate to God in their ordinary lives through our groups and studies and relevant and relatable teachings. We are always finding creative ways to help people gather and connect, to share their stories and lives with others when on campus. They become committed and faithful when they discover a ministry or a need that matches their gifts, passion, and purpose. We are constantly addressing this in all that we do, to ensure people know we hear them and see them and know what they need.

Recommending. Exponential—and accelerated—growth happens in the life of a local church when that church is recommended. Recommending seems so simple but like riding a bike takes practice to master. The results can be contagious. Here is a recent conversation between me (Jim) and my son-in-law when he told me about the church they are now attending in the Austin area:

Son-in law: "We don't go to our old United Methodist church anymore. We liked it okay, but we love our new church. Lots of people in our neighborhood go there."

Me: "I'm curious. Why did you go the first time? Did somebody invite you?"

Son-in-law: "Oh no. We just heard everybody talking about it all the time, so we decided to give it a try."

Notice it wasn't an invitation but a recommendation that resulted in my family changing churches. I'm not trashing invitations, because most researchers still proclaim that personal invitation is the most effective way of getting a neighbor or friend to attend church with you. Invitation and Recommendation are first cousins, and they are essential for a healthy culture.

Recommendation is a key growth driver for my (Yvette's) church, Impact Church, a UMC congregation in Atlanta. We make sure that our culture of "doing church differently" is reflected in our peoples' language when they're inviting and recommending the church to others. When we are asked how we have such a broad span of generations and cross sections of people, we attribute it to the same messaging about the worship experience, the casual dress, and the variety of effective ways we do church differently. That piques people's curiosity. Another characteristic of this church's culture is our online presence, which promotes the idea of recommendation and gives people the opportunity to shop us online before committing to coming in person. Our aim is for everyone, not just the pastor, to share the same understanding of our culture and what makes for a successful match with people new to us.

Growing your culture with intentionality—embedding a deep understanding of it in the staff, leaders, congregants, and the community—is most likely going to result in church growth. Often that growth is evidenced in worship, disciple-making groups, generosity, missional involvement, and spiritual depth.

Part Three

Building Your Church Culture Team

Chapter 12

The Culture Creation Team: Promote and Protect

Toxic culture is like carbon monoxide; you don't see or smell it,
but you wake up dead!
—Samuel R. Chand, *Cracking Your Church's Culture Code*

Culture has immense long-term power, for good or ill, in any organization. I (Yvette) choose to shop at one grocery store over another because of the perceived culture of each business. It is a service-focused, quality-focused, price-conscientious culture, all of which are important to me. For years I refused to shop at a large retail chain because of their toxic employee and corporate culture. In the 1990s I boycotted a gas station chain and still do to this day after it was made public the racist comments senior executives made in a board meeting. That board's attitudes spoke volumes about the culture at that company! The culture of the church is likewise being constantly assessed by the world. People are evaluating the church—just as I evaluated that retail chain and that gas station—based upon its heart, passions, and integrity. Throughout this book we have been talking about the significance of culture, especially church culture as it is created, developed, and championed by the church's leadership team. There is no question that an organization's culture sets the tone for its success.

In this chapter we'll (a) examine common ways in which any organizational culture—no matter how healthy and strong—can become fragile,

113

stagnant, irrelevant, or even toxic; and (b) focus on promoting the culture consistently while at the same time protecting the culture diligently.

Protecting: First, let's look at the importance of constantly "protecting" the church's culture. Because all cultures—even strong healthy ones—are susceptible to being weakened by apathy, inattention, or even persistent attacks from inside and outside forces that can harm it. Marcus Carlson in *Habits of Healthy Churches* observes, "Once established, a dysfuntional culture manages to easily reproduce itself often without us even noticing. Toxicity begets toxicity."[1] If the culture is becoming increasingly negative, better change the trend now rather than wait until it gets worse. One of the challenges, of course, is that often the culture is eroding away from the inside out, slowly and hidden from public view. Like the metaphor of that tall oak tree growing strong and stately for generations, and then when it falls in a storm it can be seen that inside it was rotting away. Likewise, organizations that appear strong and healthy have an uncanny way of masking what is decaying on the inside, hidden from view. That is why one purpose of a Culture Creation Team is to keep a watchful eye on the behind the scenes, interior health of the church.

How does this interior rot happen, you might ask. Do you remember Pastor Josh in chapter 8? In the three-step process he utilized, after you (1) See it, then you must (2) Embody it. The "See it" are words spoken because culture travels on words. If leaders say the culture words but do not embody them, the culture will stagnate or become irrelevant or even worse, become toxic. The final step in his process is to (3) Defend it. A church's culture may be healthy and strong, but any culture is vulnerable; one staff member or key leader who trumpets some other culture or contradictory values can ruin an otherwise healthy culture. This happens when contrary subcultures begin to arise due to weaknesses in the church's ability to articulate and live out its desired culture. "Subculture takes over like a weed. . . . Like a vegetable garden with weeds popping up, a church left unattended can allow the wrong things to grow. It is a problem of omission more than commission."[2]

My (Jim's) son, at forty years old, was a strong, healthy young man. But some random virus attacked him, settled into his spine, and turned his life upside down. He lost control of the lower half of his body. The invading virus upended not only his life but our life—as his parents—as well. He was no longer independent and needed to move in with us so we could be his caregivers.

That virus first appeared as a simple cold or flu. But it soon turned toxic. That's what viruses can do. And the same can happen in a healthy church culture. That is why it is wise to put together a culture creation team not only to promote the culture within the church but also to protect the culture from anything that can disrupt it. This often means simply to be alert and pay attention to what is happening in the church and what can be seen as emerging from the culture.

Says Sam Chand, "The question I always ask myself when I sense a troubled culture is, 'Why hasn't someone done something about it already? Don't they see it too?' The answer is no. The dysfunction in the culture has become entirely normal. It's the way things have been, and the way people assume they will always be."[3] Seemingly innocuous things—like my son's virus—can turn into a toxic invasion or attack. The attacks may be overt and well-organized, and may even come from outside the system. Many a church has been the victim of outside forces (a contrary theology, a critic of the church or denomination, some personal agenda) that somehow manage to gain a foothold of influence, and ultimately over the course of years or even decades, they do great damage.

Those kinds of attacks are what we call the church's "cowbird problem." The cowbird is a species of wild bird common in the Midwest and other parts of the country. It is unique in that it does not build a nest of its own; rather it finds a comfortable-looking nest built by some other pasture bird and co-opts it. Here is how: the momma bird seeks out an already-existing nest that may already even have eggs in it. No bother to her. She surreptitiously flies in, lays her own eggs among the others, and then flies away. Also unique to the cowbird is that she doesn't bother to do much parenting; she lets the actual owner of the nest unknowingly do that for her. The eggs our cowbird lays look so similar to the resident eggs that the nest owner following its natural instincts can't tell the difference and nurses the eggs and then the newborn fledglings. The only difference, also unknown to her, is that the gestation period of the cowbird's eggs will be a few days less than her own species.

So what happens is that the cowbird's eggs hatch before the other eggs. Plus, the cowbird young is a bigger, more demanding hatchling. Even after the original eggs hatch, the cowbird chicks aggressively squawk louder and receive more of the food the owner birds bring to their nest. And to top it off, the cowbird hatchlings grow faster, aggressively bullying the other chicks for position and food. The result is that the cowbird literally kicks the other birds out of their own nest. They take it over. It is nature's amazing show of treachery: the cowbird contributes nothing, is fed by parents not its own, and when the time is right, simply flies away with no responsibilities. It is a demonstration of "the one who is the loudest bully often gets their way."

We frequently see this dynamic at play in politics or the corporate world. But sadly it is alive and well in churches too. If a church does not guard and protect its culture, someone who appears well-meaning can get into the system, sneak into leadership, and end up taking over the church with their loud and bullying tactics before you know it. It is not rare for a church to have a cowbird problem. Does yours? The best way to avoid the cowbird problem is with a strong, healthy culture, not only promoted constantly and continually but also protected from all sorts of attacks, whether they first appear as treacherous or not. Some attacks on the healthy body of the church may also be almost accidental. They begin slowly and innocently. Maybe no one person is in charge or even aware of what is happening, but that is the problem: no one is responsible for protecting the culture. The assumption is "that could never happen here," and so there is no intentionality about keeping the culture strong and healthy.

But be careful how you go about assigning people or a team to promote and protect the culture and how you define their responsibility. Observes Roger Conners in *Change the Culture, Change the Game*: "You might be tempted to appoint a 'chief culture officer,' but that would just rob the leadership team of one of its most vital responsibilities. . . . Culture building will and must involve every single leader in your organization."[4] Culture allows for church growth when every leader—pastors, staff, key leaders, various leadership teams, program heads, class teachers, volunteers in servant ministries and missions, influencers—gladly takes on the role of promoting the culture, messaged through the leadership's culture words.

Promoting the culture is the responsibility of every stakeholder, but it is modeled by the church's pastor and key leaders. William Vanderbloemen, longtime church staffing specialist, observes in *Culture Wins*: "The more the leaders live out the culture, the more employees will follow suit. If the leader embodies, pushes, and champions culture, participates with team members, and is visible and accessible, the culture will thrive."[5]

The messaging of the culture—once identified and promoted—is what keeps it alive and strong; it must be done intentionally and consistently throughout all layers of the church population covering the pastors, staff, core leaders, key volunteers, those highly involved, marginally involved, minimally involved and not involved (solely consumers). Care must be taken to ensure culture messaging reaches and resonates with all stakeholders.

Kevin Gerald echoes his thought in talking about whether your culture is by design, or by default: "A culture by default is old and fixed. . . . But a created culture is always evolving."[6] A culture "by default" tends to be that unexamined culture that the current iteration of a congregation has just inherited over the years. It encapsulates an attitude of "The way we've always done things," and just exists within your church in ways that often hold it back.

So we recommend—in good Wesleyan style—assembling a culture creation team. Empower and enthuse that team by following this simple rule of thumb: to create great culture, go to great culture! Encourage your Culture Creation Team to take field trips to places in your community known for their great culture. Theaters, sports stadiums, restaurants, churches, businesses, and so on. Then debrief when you return: What stood out to you? What about the culture drew you in? What did you admire? What would you improve? The team will begin to develop a radar for great culture, and for what threatens it.

In summary, the Culture Creation Team's work is a dual-pronged focus: One focus is **promoting** the culture in good, healthy ways. Gracefully and intentionally being sure the culture words and their impact are evident in church activities, events, and lifestyle. For instance, if a culture word is "fun," the team would help make sure that there are seasonal events that are truly fun! Trunk or Treat and Church Anniversary celebrations will be infused with lots of things that attendees will say, "That sure was fun!" If a culture word is "caring," the team will be asking how various ministries in the church clearly convey care. The team wouldn't necessarily be directly involved with care ministries, but they would be asking how leadership is ensuring that good systems of congregational care are in place and evident.

The other focus is **protecting** the culture from atrophy, apathy, or ambush by people or events that are counterculture. It must stay relentless in defending against attacks that might come via people or practices that threaten the culture's vitality and clarity.

To help guide the work of the team, take a look at the Action Plan Quadrant on the next page.

The church culture team is not to "lord it over" anybody. Team members should not become or be perceived as the "culture police" who act as the judge and jury of every aspect of the church's life. Rather you want the team to operate in a spirit of servanthood and mentorship working side-by-side with the lead pastor and other church leaders. The job of the culture creation team is not to change the culture; that is the responsibility of the core leadership of the church. Its job is to pay attention to the practices and attitudes of the church to ensure they align with the professed culture. The team will not be large—just a handful of good-hearted, like-minded people assembled by the pastor and key leaders. Some churches and organizations refer to this team as culture ambassadors whose mission is to show the culture at gatherings, celebrations, and within the everyday life of the church.

CHURCH CULTURE CHANGE
Action PLAN QUADRANT

CHALLENGES   **OPPORTUNITIES**

Clarity on our desired results?   Actions (we) can take to assess, change, &
"What keeps us from achieving them?"   create culture.

GOALS   **PLANS**

SMART goals; immediate & long term desired results   Be specific; steps to SEE IT, SAY IT, SHOW IT, GROW IT

D**I**FFERENCE
MAKERS

Let's review: (1) As the lead pastor you have seen the importance of making your church's culture your top priority. (2) As the lead pastor you have begun the journey of finding your personal culture words. (3) You are putting together a culture team made up of trusted church leaders who demonstrate a nonthreatening approach to digging deep into the life of the church they love. (4) You have worked with this team regarding the best ways to solicit assessment information in keeping with practices of the church. (5) To be intentional and to stay on strategy, you and your team are being guided by the Action Plan Quadrant.

Keep in mind that not many church people are adept at all about what *culture change* even means. The scary word is not *culture* but *change*. As is often said in various ways, "people do not resist change, they resist being changed." Because of this truism, in our process we recommend that the church avoid making culture change some kind of big program or process. Resist the temptation to hang banners on the wall or create catchy posters with the pastor's culture words. This process is not intended to become the church's next big emphasis. Rather, follow the steps in this process and let it become an organic, contagious culture shift within the church. In the language of the biblical story of Elisha, it is generally not necessary to make a big splash or even stir things up: just make little ripples of influence to see the miracle of culture change happen in your church.

A suggested good practice for the team to follow is the "list and enlist" approach. This simply involves keeping an ongoing list of the concrete values that church leadership believes form the foundation of the preferred culture of the church. As the list plays out in daily behaviors and practices, the team would help focus leaders to keep asking: Are they biblical? Are they positive? Are they aligned with the culture of the denomination? And then the team would enlist buy-in from other leaders and stake holders. How? By encouraging and arranging timely, healthy dialogue and discussion.[7] Remember that creating culture, and maintaining it is not a one and done thing. It takes repetition in a positive and productive environment. Your culture team will be essential in ensuring you have the culture you want to get the results you desire.

Chapter 13

Conclusion: The City Mouse and the Country Mouse

"In a healthy culture trust is more common and natural. Love more easily expressed, and it is expressed and experienced on a deeper level."
—Marcus J. Carlson, *Habits of Healthy Churches*

A few days ago, I received an email with this simple yet intriguing header: "You've Made a Difference." The email went on to explain, "Your purchase ensures a pair of glasses will be distributed to someone in need. A big, big Thank You for your purchase!" Warby Parker sells eyewear and has long been recognized for its great culture. I experienced this culture firsthand when—after numerous failed attempts to get my prescription filled in a satisfactory way—I went to a Warby Parker store. I had to drive a ways, but it was well worth it. The store exuded hospitality, customer service, and an inviting environment based on their familiar library motif. No pushy salesman, just helpful guidance done in great fashion. Plus, both the regular eyeglasses and the sunglasses I purchased were of high quality and had lower prices than I found elsewhere. The price, however, is not what sold me. As Yvette observed earlier, it was the culture. As a bonus, after the purchase I learned that I had "made a difference." And who doesn't want to make a difference? I felt good leaving the store (no buyers remorse) and even better when I received the follow-up email.

"Making a difference" is a target of any good culture, especially a church culture. Hopefully this book has shown you ways to communicate to your church and to guests that through your ministry people can and do

121

make a difference. You have seen that—such as with Warby Parker—your church's culture is often the deciding factor for a first-time guest to return. It is not what you do (lots of places sell eyewear in-store or online); it is how you go about doing what you do that makes the difference. In *Change the Culture, Change the Game*, Roger Conners and Tom Smith demonstrate the three levels of change: temporary change (to meet or rectify an immediate need), transitional change (incremental change for a season), and transformational change (long-term, long-lasting significant change).[1] In the church world, we see this around some pastoral transition situations: A pastor leaves unexpectedly from a struggling church and an interim is installed (temporary). There is the example of a church that goes through our changeover zone process of receiving a new pastor (transitional). But unless the church follows through with longer-term systemic and cultural changes to go side by side with receiving a new pastor (transformational), the church will not take advantage of opportunities in front of them.

Hopefully through reading this book you see that our interest is in transformational cultural change. In reading this book you have learned how to understand and assess your church's current culture. You have realized that your church's culture is your top priority, and you have gained insights and explored tools for both changing and creating the culture you and your leadership want so that it can achieve the desired results your church needs. You have seen how to go about establishing some sort of culture creation team whose main purpose is to work closely with every leadership group in the church to intentionally promote and protect the culture of your church. Hopefully you agree that your culture brings about the transformational change that is so important for any church today. As we read the stories of the Bible, Genesis to Revelation, there is great emphasis placed on describing the culture of the day because the culture had such an influence on the decisions, behaviors, and trajectory of the lives of those living in those times and their relationship with God.

Culture, on every level and in every place on earth, has continued to change—influenced by major events or shifts in leadership, perspectives, technology, and the passing of time. As an African American woman, I (Yvette) think about my own family history and all the culture shifts that have affected my journey and my relationship with the church. My life has been disrupted, shaped, and improved by the shifts in the prevailing cultures that make up American history; from the prevailing culture during slavery and the transatlantic slave trade and the civil rights era, to the social media culture, and even by the shifts in church culture seen in televangelist teaching, prosperity gospel, Christian nationalism, and the list goes on.

As we draw the book to its conclusion, I hope we can agree that culture is a significant "influencer" in our world, our corporations, our homes, schools, and yes, our churches. Yet, the need for proactively and intentionally establishing and maintaining the internal culture is often overlooked, underestimated, undeveloped, and under-managed, which limits our effectiveness to live fully into our goals, mission, vision, dreams, and desired results.

Social media and our world's ever-expanding technology have spurred an awakening to the importance of culture. Culture is our largest influencer of people, companies, and our churches. Culture has become a prevalent topic, and people everywhere are now aware of not only culture in general, but subcultures too. Cancel culture, Me Too, Black Lives Matter, and environmental culture movements are continually springing forth, and they influence corporations, institutions, and the church. These organizations increasingly recognize the need to understand culture and to establish and manage it wisely.

For centuries children have learned Aesop's fable of the city mouse and the country mouse. Its popularity has enabled it to be adapted for new audiences in new ways throughout the decades: from oral storytelling, to cartoons, to children's books, and even to a movie and television series in the 1990s. The moral of the story has been extrapolated in countless views; its meanings can be and have been interpreted in a number of clever and sometimes even controversial ways.

But one thing is abundantly clear: It is a fable about culture. Each mouse determines their respective values, practices, behaviors, and preferences based on culture. That's what culture does: it aligns our preferences, practices, behaviors, habits, routines, and values. Do you remember the story? A country mouse invited a cousin from the city to visit. The city mouse was not impressed with the sparse diet of his cousin, so he invited his cousin to the city. There they enjoyed a wide variety of incredible food stuffs, but they also had to contend with the scary cat and imposing humans. So the country mouse heads back, saying he prefers the scarcity of the country to the scariness of the city.

Two creatures are doing about the same thing—nibbling—but doing it in totally different ways based on the unique culture of each mouse. Each mouse was a product of the culture in which it lived, and the culture in which they lived made a difference in how each one lived. But this short course on church culture is more than a fable about the culture in which we live; it is about the culture that lives within your church. Now that you've learned the importance of being intentional in creating the culture which lives within you and your church, the culture that reflects and shapes your values, habits, practices, attitudes, and daily routines of "how we go about doing what we do around here."

You get a choice in what culture you want to have, and that choice makes a difference. Remember from Elisha's story: it isn't about making a big splash or stirring things up; It's just little ripples of influence done repeatedly and done well. What we are saying is, "Thank God, you can create a culture that makes a difference!" And that connects!

The Ultimate Culture Is One That Connects

As the founder and strategist at Wisdom & Wit, I (Yvette) consult with businesses and churches of all sizes, shapes, and ethnicities, and I coach their leaders. When I learn of their mission and vision, I immediately begin to evaluate if their actual culture matches the clients, customers, and audience they wish to reach. The best marketing leaders get this, which is why today's products market to a community based on a specific culture or culture's behavior, or pattern of belief. I remember the pressure my boys put on me when everyone in our family had an iPhone and I did not. They hated sending me messages because it broke the connected community of messaging within a group as a family. It was culturally important that we be a family and be connected, even when texting. At my next phone upgrade, I got an iPhone. Apple has done a phenomenal job creating a need for community but also feeding our innate cultural need for connection. Their devices make calls and send text messages—they facilitate our communication, but *how* we communicate with these devices, in ways that foster continual connection—this has been the game changer. The "how" is crucial. It is no different when I consult with churches to help them increase their reach to make more disciples for Jesus Christ.

You can walk into a thousand different churches and none of them will be exactly the same. People choose to be part of this church or that church precisely because of the differences they perceive from church to church, and the qualities they experience. United Methodist churches use the same hymnals and preach from the same Bible and yet each church is distinct. You might visit several in the same city, and ultimately choose *the* one for you. I can attend a predominantly African American United Methodist Church and worship God, experience the preaching of the gospel of Jesus Christ and experience the movement of the Holy Spirit differently than if I attend a predominantly Anglo-Saxon Eurocentric church. This testifies to the significance of culture. By the way, though they are very different culturally, because of the presence of Christ, I can enjoy both equally but in different ways.

Too often in church leadership, the focus is more on what worship will look like or the programs and events we will host, rather than "how we go about doing all that we do," which is what attracts people in the first place. The Bible advised us of this when it stated in John 13:34-35, "*A new command I give you: Love one another. As I have loved you, so you must love one another. By this everyone will know that you are my disciples, if you love one another*" (NIV). Jesus did not only emphasize the "what" but more importantly the "how." *How* we become the church, *how* we love those in the communities around us, and *how* we engage in life with one another is what makes a church's culture—which is what draws people to the church.

If you want to grow the ministry of your church, you have to connect the culture of the church to Jesus Christ and then thrust it outward for all the world to see. What does the Bible say? "Apart from Him we can do nothing" (John 15:5 NIV). People who attend your church, visit your church, lead in your church, and work in your church want to see the connection that the church provides from God to their everyday ordinary lives! How you do that is directly tied to the culture you create and maintain within the church. I love the lyrics in Edgar Guest's poem, "Sermons We See." The most famous line is "I'd rather see a sermon than to hear one any day." But I really love, "For I might misunderstand you and the high advice you give, but there's no misunderstanding how you act and how you live." In other words, *I want to see how you do it* rather than hear you tell me. If you want to see a ministry happening in your church outside of Sunday, the pathway to success is made by creating a cultural connection that connects to Christ. This is the kind of culture that must intentionally be promoted, and it must diligently be protected.

We have included two additional tools, The Complete Culture Audit and Eleven Laws of Church Culture, online at www.abingdonpress .com/culture-extras. These powerful resources for your church's culture work are free and downloadable tools to share with your culture team.

Thank you for taking this journey of creating the culture you want in your church. In most cases, regardless of the situation your church finds itself in, you can discover the joy of culture change and creation.

In Texas we often remind ourselves of the "code of the rodeo," which says humbly and confidently: "There ain't a horse that can't be rode, and there ain't a rider that can't be throwed." Be confident yet humble. If you need help, let us know and we'll do whatever we can at the Difference Makers Group to assist you.

Some years ago the church I (Jim) pastored for eighteen years built a magnificent new sanctuary. At the time, it was the largest building in Flower Mound, Texas. The opening of the state-of-the-art facility was a big deal: the mayors of all the surrounding communities were there; the state senator was part of the festivities; the bishop and the district superintendent played key roles; other dignitaries were included. It was such a big deal that I flew my mother in from Springfield, Illinois, so she could see that her little boy who had gone to the big city had done well. I looked out into the full house and spotted her. She was glowing as all the muckety-mucks stood along the front of the worship center and all the clergy were decked out in our finest ecclesiastical gear.

When the morning had ended Mom and I got a few minutes alone in my home. I took my tie off, kicked up my feet on the coffee table, looked over at her, and asked, "Well, Mom, what'd you think?"

And as only a mother could say, without hesitation, she deadpanned: "I thought your pant legs were too long."

Well friends, if you read through these many pages, I hope it didn't sound like we have been telling you "your pant legs are too long." You all lead outstanding churches, doing amazing work. Our hope is that we've shared with you some ways to increase your impact and to focus your efforts for more fruitfulness.

The good news is that when a church changes its culture (the micro-culture) so that it can grow, then it expands its influence and becomes more intentional about being a difference maker. Then the church changes the culture of the community and the world around it (the macroculture). We close with those powerful words of Scripture that remind us that culture change and creating something new is not solely the province of our clever planning and strategic planning: "And the one who was seated on the throne said, 'See, I am making all things new'" (Rev 21:5 NRSVUE).

Afterword

By Jim Chandler, Lead Strategist, Difference Makers

Thank you for considering this journey of culture change and creation! It is true that "an important principle of creating a healthy culture is becoming comfortable with some unresolved issues."[1] So if you still have questions, and most likely you're dealing right now with unresolved issues in your church, don't worry! A healthy culture allows for that space of uncertainty. Dealing with problems, not answering them all, is the stuff of moving forward as a church.

As I mentioned in the foreword, I enjoy riding my Harley-Davidson motorcycle. One of the unique cultural aspects of riding a Harley is picking up poker chips at dealerships. Wherever a Harley rider goes anywhere in the world, we make a point of picking up chips at every dealership that is unique to the town or city we are in. Riders have amazing collections, and each chip is a memorial to a particular ride.

We hope this book has been a good experience, and we hope that this brief stop off in your journey on the way to building a God-honoring church won't be just to pick up another momento, but rather to create momentum for building an amazing culture that will make possible many marker moments for your congregation.

Jim Ozier's contributions to this book are from the perspective of a long-tenured clergy; Yvette Thibodeaux's contributions come from the perspective of a lay person, dedicated to her church in particular and the church in general. She brings her business acumen to bear in the church world in a timely way. One of her family's favorite sayings it, "chew the meat and spit out the bone!" And we hope that is the way you have digested this book: Keep, use, and enjoy what has been helpful; spit out what is irrelevant to your situation.

As I stated at the start of this short course on church culture, "Changing the culture is not a leisurely Sunday afternoon drive through pleasant scenery in the comfort of "we've always done it this way." Instead, it is often a wild and unpredictable trip into places unknown and yet to be explored. It can be full of exhilaration and risks, detours and setbacks, dangers and thrills."

In the meantime, our prayers are with you as you integrate this short course on culture into the life of your church. Remember that it starts with clarity on your desired results. Your desired results can be for a season; they don't have to be for eternity (though one of your desired results may be to get people ready for eternity!).

Is it time for a culture checkup? Look again at the culture checkup tool. A multitude of factors may beg for a checkup. If it's time, it's time. So do it!

Remember that the single most important word in assessing, creating, or changing culture is *intentionality*. If what you have read in this short course seems to work for you, go for it! If it doesn't seem right for your setting, let your own creativity and intentionality guide you to getting to your desired results.

If you are not getting the results you desire, change the culture!

Bibliography

Cited Resources

Blandino, Stephen. *Creating Your Church's Culture: How to Uproot Mediocrity and Create a Healthy Organizational Culture*. Self-published, 2013.

Carlson, Marcus J. *Habits of Healthy Churches: 7 Practices to Transform Your Church's Culture*. Self-published, 2022.

Chand, Samuel R. *Cracking Your Church's Culture Code: Seven Keys to Unleashing Vision and Inspiration*. Leadership Network. San Francisco: Jossey-Bass, 2011.

Connors, Roger and Tom Smith. *Change the Culture, Change the Game*. New York: Portfolio/Penguin, 2011.

Gerald, Kevin. *By Design or Default: Creating a Church Culture That Works*. Nashville: Thomas Nelson, 2006.

Grierson, Denham. *Transforming a People of God*. Melbourne Joint Board of Christian Education, 1984.

Harper, Steve. *Five Marks of a Methodist: The Fruit of a Living Faith*. Nashville: Abingdon Press, 2015.

Jeary, Tony. *Results Faster! 7 Proven Principles to Personal & Professional Mastery*. Franklin, TN: Clovercroft, 2016.

Job, Rueben P. *Three Simple Rules: A Wesleyan Way of Living*. Nashville: Abingdon Press, 2007.

Lencioni, Patrick. *The Advantage*. San Francisco: Jossey-Bass, 2012.

Lewis, Robert, and Wayne Cordeiro. *Culture Shift: Transforming Your Church from the Inside*. Leadership Network. New York: Jossey-Bass, 2005.

Malphurs, Aubrey. *Look Before You Lead: How to Discern and Shape Your Church Culture*. Grand Rapids: Baker Books, 2013.

Meador, Jake. "The Misunderstood Reason Millions Stopped Going to Church," *Washington Post* (July 29, 2023).

Morgan, Tony. *The Unstuck Church: Equipping Churches to Experience Sustained Health*. Leadership Network. Nashville: Thomas Nelson, 2017.

Ozier, Jim. *Clip In: Risking Hospitality in Your Church*. Nashville: Abingdon Press, 2014.

Ozier, Jim and Jim Griffith. *The Changeover Zone: Successful Pastoral Transitions*. Nashville: Abingdon Press, 2016.

Schaller, Lyle. *The New Pastor*. Nashville: Abingdon Press, 1988.

Schein, Edgar H. *Organizational Culture and Leadership*, 2nd ed. San Francisco: Jossey-Bass, 1999.

Spore, Roy L. *Productive Ministry: A Guide for Ministry in the Small Church*. Eugene, OR: Wipf and Stock, 2021.

Vanderbloemen, Will. *Culture Wins: The Roadmap to an Irresistible Workplace*. New York: Savio Republic Books: 2018.

Weems, Lovett H. Jr. *Church Leadership: Vision, Team, Culture, and Integrity*. Nashville: Abingdon Press, 2010.

Further Reading

Chatman, J.A. and K.A. Jehn. "Assessing the relationship between industry characteristics and organizational culture: How different can you be?" *Academy of Management Journal* 37 (1994): 522–53.

Deal, Terrence E., and Allan A. Kennedy. *Corporate Cultures: The Rites and Rituals of Corporate Life*. Reading, MA: Addison-Wesley, 1982.

Graf, Alan B. "Building Corporate Cultures." *Chief Executive*. March 2005, 18.

Hofstede, Geert. *Cultures and Organizations: Software of the Mind*. New York: McGraw-Hill, 1991.

LaRue, Bruce, and Robert R. Ivany. "Transform Your Culture." *Executive Excellence*, December 2004, 14–15.

LeFranc, Fred. "A Dynamic Culture Can Make a Franchise System Successful." *Franchising World*, February 2005, 75–77.

Lencioni, Patrick. *The Advantage: Why Organizational Health Trumps Everything Else in Business*. San Francisco: Jossey-Bass, 2012.

Loehr, Jim, and Tony Schwartz. *The Power of Full Engagement: Managing Energy Not Time Is the Key to High Performance and Personal Renewal*. New York: Simon & Shuster, 2003.

Niebuhr, H. Richard. *Christ and Culture*. Harper Collins; 1951, updated 1996.

Wren, J. Thomas *The Leaders Companion: Insights on Leadership Through the Ages*. New York: The Free Press, 1995.

Notes

Introduction

1. Lovett H. Weems, Jr., *Church Leadership: Vision, Team, Culture, and Integrity* (Nashville: Abingdon Press, 2010), 84.

1. Why Another Book on Church Culture?

Epigraph: Tony Morgan, *The Unstuck Church: Equipping Churches to Experience Sustained Health,* Leadership Network (Nashville: Thomas Nelson, 2017), 51.

1. Samuel R. Chand, *Cracking Your Church's Culture Code: Seven Keys to Unleashing Vision and Inspiration*, Leadership Network (San Francisco: Jossey-Bass, 2011), 2.

2. Stephen Blandino, *Creating Your Church's Culture: How to Uproot Mediocrity and Create a Healthy Organizational Culture* (self-published, 2013), 12.

3. Jenni Caldron in the online Culture Conference 2022.

4. Heather Zemple in the online Culture Conference 2022.

5. Edgar H. Schein, *Organizational Culture and Leadership,* 2nd ed. (San Francisco: Jossey-Bass, 1999), 6.

6. Andy Crouch, Kurt Keilhacker, and Dave Blanchard, "Leading Beyond the Blizzard" (blog and podcast), https://journal.praxislabs.org /leading-beyond-the-blizzard-why-every-organization-is-now-a-startup -b7f32fb278ff. The article is written "especially for leaders of businesses and nonprofit organizations who are fellow Christians, because Christians of all people are equipped to face the current reality with both clear-eyed realism and unparalleled hope. . . . From today onward, most leaders must

recognize that the business they were in no longer exists. This applies not just to for-profit businesses, but to nonprofits, and even in certain important respects to churches."

7. Chand, *Cracking Your Church's Culture Code*, 113.

8. Rueben P. Job, *Three Simple Rules: A Wesleyan Way of Living* (Nashville: Abingdon Press, 2007).

9. See, for instance, research blog post by Wesleyan Scholar Dr. Kevin Watson, "Wesley Didn't Say It: Do all the good you can, by all the means you can . . . ," https://kevinmwatson.com/2013/04/29/wesley-didnt-say-it -do-all-the-good-you-can-by-all-the-means-you-can/ (April 29, 2013).

2. Church Culture: What It Is and What It Isn't

Epigraph: Samuel R. Chand, *Cracking Your Church's Culture Code; Seven Keys to Unleashing Vision & Inspiration*, Leadership Network (San Francisco: Jossey-Bass, 2011), 11.

1. Lovett Weems, *Church Leadership: Vision, Team, Culture, and Integrity* (Nashville: Abingdon, 2010), 82, 83.

2. Denham Grierson, *Transforming a People of God* (Melbourne Joint Board of Christian Education, 1984), 34; quoted in Weems, *Church Leadership*, 83.

3. Stephen Bandino, *Creating Your Church's Culture: How to Uproot Mediocrity and Create a Healthy Organizational Culture* (self-published, 2013), 11.

3. Church Culture: Your Top Priority

Epigraph: Kevin Gerald, *By Design or Default: Creating a Church Culture That Works* (Nashville: Thomas Nelson, 2006), 7.

1. Marcus J. Carlson, *Habits of Healthy Churches: 7 Practices to Transform Your Church's Culture* (self-published, 2022), 34.

2. Patrick Lencioni, *The Advantage* (New York: Jossey-Bass, 2012), 3.

3. Roy L. Spore, "Understanding and Honoring Your Congregation's Unique Culture," Lewis Center for Church Leadership, https://www.

churchleadership.com/leading-ideas/understanding-and-honoring-your
-congregations-unique-culture/ (July 12, 2022), based on Roy's book, *Productive Ministry: A Guide for Ministry in the Small Church* (Eugene, OR: Wipf and Stock, 2021).

4. Planting Culture in a New Church Start

Epigraph: Stephen Bandino, *Creating Your Church's Culture: How to Uproot Mediocrity and Create a Healthy Organizational Culture* (self-published, 2013), 21.

1. Jake Meador, "The Misunderstood Reason Millions Stopped Going to Church," *Washington Post* (July 29, 2023). Meador cites recent research of over seven thousand Americans by Ryan Burge and Paul Djupe, the book *The Great Dechurching* by Jim Davis and Michael Graham, and other similar work by Tim Keller.

2. Meador, "The Misunderstood Reason Millions Stopped Going to Church."

3. Tony Jeary, *Results Faster! 7 Proven Principles to Personal & Professional Mastery* (Franklin, TN: Clovercroft, 2016), 152.

4. Aubrey Malphurs, *Look Before You Lead: How to Discern and Shape Your Church Culture* (Grand Rapids: Baker Books, 2013), 48.

5. For a case study on this sad reality, see the *Christianity Today* podcast, "The Rise and Fall of Mars Hill," hosted by Mike Cosper in June 2021. As the written teaser states: "Founded in 1996, Seattle's Mars Hill Church was poised to be an influential, undeniable force in evangelicalism—that is until it spiraling collapse in 2014. The church and its charismatic leader, Mark Driscoll, had a promising start. But the perils of power, conflict, and Christian celebrity eroded and eventually shipwrecked both the preacher and his multi-million dollar platform" (https://www.christianitytoday.com/ct/podcasts/rise-and-fall-of-mars-hill/).

6. Robert Lewis and Wayne Cordeiro, *Culture Shift: Transforming Your Church from the Inside*, Leadership Network publication (San Francisco: Jossey-Bass, 2005), 106. Over the years Lewis and Cordeiro have been major ambassadors for elevating the study, practice, and creation of a healthy culture as a focus of leadership. The authors proclaim without apology the importance of their church's culture: "We both make it our number one priority to manage and protect the culture of the church" (page xxiii).

5. Principles of Assessing Church Culture

Epigraph: Marcus Carlson, *Habits of Healthy Churches: 7 Practices to Transform Your Church's Culture* (self-published, 2022), 12.

1. Aubrey Malphurs, *Look Before You Lead: How to Discern and Shape Your Church Culture* (Grand Rapids: Baker Books, 2013), 21.

2. Roger Conners and Tom Smith, *Change the Culture, Change the Game* (New York: Portfolio/Penguin, 2011), 18.

6. Tools for Assessing Your Church Culture

Epigraph: Edgar H. Schein, *Organizational Culture and Leadership*, 2nd ed. (San Francisco: Jossey-Bass, 1999).

7. "See It, Say It, Show It, Grow It" Overview

Epigraph: Roger Connors and Tom Smith, *Change the Culture, Change the Game* (New York: Portfolio/Penguin, 2011).

1. Tony Jeary, *Results Faster! 7 Proven Principles to Personal & Professional Mastery* (Franklin, TN: Clovercroft, 2016), 109.

2. Jim Ozier and Jim Griffith, *The Changeover Zone: Successful Pastoral Transitions* (Nashville: Abingdon Press, 2016).

3. Lyle Schaller, *The New Pastor* (Nashville: Abingdon Press, 1988), 39.

8. See It: Finding Your Culture Words

Epigraph: Stephen Blandino, *Creating Your Church's Culture: How to Uproot Mediocrity and Create a Healthy Organizational Culture* (self-published, 2013), 11.

1. Aubrey Malphurs, *Look Before You Lead: How to Discern and Shape Your Church Culture* (Grand Rapids: Baker Books, 2013), 20.

2. Bob Smietana, *Church Leaders*, "United Methodist Pastors Feel Worse and Worry More Than a Decade Ago," August 11, 2023, https://julieroys.com/united-methodist-pastors-feel-worse-worry-more-than-decade-ago/.

3. William Vanderbloemen, *Culture Wins: The Roadmap to an Irresistable Workplace* (New York: Savio Republic Books; 2018), 12.

4. Aubrey Malphurs, for instance, devotes an entire chapter in his *Look Before You Lead* book to "Discovering the Pastor's Culture" (page 97ff.).

9. Say It: Threading Your Culture Words

Epigraph: Robert Lewis and Wayne Cordeiro, *Culture Shift: Transforming Your Church from the Inside*, Leadership Network (New York: Jossey-Bass, 2005), 41.

1. Marcus Carlson, *Habits of Healthy Churches: 7 Practices to Transform Your Church Culture* (self-published, 2022), 50.

2. Steve Harper, *Five Marks of a Methodist: The Fruit of a Living Faith* (Nashville: Abingdon Press, 2015).

10. Show It: Spreading Your Culture Words

Epigraph: Marcus J. Carlson, *Habits of Healthy Churches: 7 Practices to Transform Your Church's Culture* (self-published, 2022), 33.

1. Kevin Gerald, *By Design or Default: Creating a Church Culture That Works* (Nashville: Thomas Nelson, 2006), 60, 61.

2. Edgar H. Schein, *Organizational Culture and Leadership*, 2nd ed. (San Francisco: Jossey-Bass, 1999), 248–50.

3. Lovett Weems, *Church Leadership: Vision, Team, Culture, and Integrity* (Nashville: Abingdon Press, 2010), 90–95.

11. Grow It: Embedding Culture in the Congregation

Epigraph: Robert Lewis and Wayne Cordeiro, *Culture Shift: Transforming Your Church from the Inside*, Leadership Network (New York: Jossey-Bass, 2005), 45.

1. Will Vanderbloemen, *Culture Wins: The Roadmap to an Irresistible Workplace* (New York: Savio Republic Books, 2018), 8.

2. Much of the material in this section is a revised version from material in my (Jim's) book, *Clip In: Risking Hospitality in Your Church* (Nashville: Abingdon Press, 2014), chapters 7–10.

3. Roger Connors and Tom Smith, *Change the Culture, Change the Game* (New York: Portfolio/Penguin, 2011).

12. The Culture Creation Team: Promote and Protect

Epigraph: Samuel R. Chand, *Cracking Your Church's Culture Code: Seven Keys to Unleashing Vision and Inspiration*, Leadership Network (San Francisco: Jossey-Bass, 2011), 12.

1. Marcus J. Carlson, *Habits of Healthy Churches: 7 Practices to Transform Your Church's Culture* (self-published, 2022).

2. Robert Lewis and Wayne Cordeiro, *Culture Shift: Transforming Your Church from the Inside*, Leadership Network (San Francisco: Jossey-Bass, 2005), 107.

3. Chand, *Cracking Your Church's Culture Code*, 21.

4. Roger Connors and Tom Smith, *Change the Culture, Change the Game* (New York: Portfolio/Penguin, 2011), 28.

5. Will Vanderbloemen, *Culture Wins: The Roadmap to an Irresistible Workplace* (New York: Savio Republic Books, 2018), 71.

6. Kevin Gerald, *By Design or Default: Creating a Church Culture That Works* (Nashville: Thomas Nelson, 2006), 24.

7. Lewis and Cordeiro, *Culture Shift*, 61.

13. Conclusion: The City Mouse and the Country Mouse

Epigraph: Marcus J. Carlson, *Habits of Healthy Churches: 7 Practices to Transform Your Church's Culture* (self-published, 2022), 39.

1. Roger Connors and Tom Smith, *Change the Culture, Change the Game* (New York: Portfolio/Penguin, 2011), 53–54.

Afterword

1. Samuel R. Chand, *Cracking Your Church's Culture Code: Seven Keys to Unleashing Vision and Inspiration*, Leadership Network (San Francisco: Jossey-Bass, 2011), 78.

Printed in the USA
CPSIA information can be obtained
at www.ICGtesting.com
LVHW032310270724
786434LV00006B/29